Hellenic Studies 65

DIALOGUING IN LATE ANTIQUITY

The baptistery of the cathedral at Nisibis (Nusaybin), today known as the Church of Mor Yaqub (see Keser-Kayaalp and Erdoğan 2013). Between the late fifth and seventh centuries the east Syrian "School" of Nisibis produced a long series of debaters, whose training included Aristotelian logic (Becker 2006).
Photo: James Pettifer, 2013.

DIALOGUING IN LATE ANTIQUITY

AVERIL CAMERON

CENTER FOR HELLENIC STUDIES
Trustees for Harvard University
Washington, D.C.
Distributed by Harvard University Press
Cambridge, Massachusetts, and London, England
2014

Dialoguing in Late Antiquity
    by Averil Cameron
Copyright © 2014 Center for Hellenic Studies, Trustees for Harvard University
All Rights Reserved.
Published by Center for Hellenic Studies, Trustees for Harvard University, Washington,
    D.C.
Distributed by Harvard University Press, Cambridge, Massachusetts, and London,
    England
Production: Ivy Livingston
Cover design: Joni Godlove
Printed by Edwards Brothers, Inc., Ann Arbor, MI

LIBRARY OF CONGRESS CATALOGING-IN-PUBLICATION DATA

Cameron, Averil
    Dialoguing in Late Antiquity / by Averil Cameron.
        p. cm. — (Hellenic Studies Series ; 65)
Catalog in Publication data available from the Library of Congress
    ISBN 978-0-674-42835-5 (alk. paper)

Everything is in a way less deep and deeper than you think. You want a long explanation, but in the end your explanation repeats what you knew at the start. You said yourself it was like remembering.

Socrates to Plato
Iris Murdoch "Art and Eros: A Dialogue About Art"

Amongst the unhappy delusions of mankind is the belief that a dispute can be settled by a debate.

Steven Runciman *The Eastern Schism*, 108

Contents

Preface

THIS BOOK TAKES UP AN INTEREST in the early use of the dialogue form by Christians that was first kindled over twenty years ago. The subject was subsequently overtaken by other pressures and other interests, until it was revived with the appearance of Simon Goldhill's provocative collection, *The End of Dialogue in Antiquity* (Goldhill 2009). Since 1991, when I published an early paper on dialogues as well as my book, *Christianity and the Rhetoric of Empire* (Averil Cameron 1991a, 1991b), and in the light of the "linguistic turn", there has been a veritable deluge of writing about early Christian literature, but not so far about early Christian prose dialogues. Neither the recent flurry of publications about the literature of "questions and answers" (*erotapokriseis*) nor the attention given, principally by Syriacists, to the verse dialogues in Syriac, which gave rise indirectly to my paper of 1991, have caused scholars to extend their range to consider as a group the large number of works written by Christians in late antiquity in the form of prose dialogues (though there are of course some excellent studies of individual works). There are indeed questions to be asked about possible connections between these different types of dialogue-writing, as well as with the many embedded dialogues contained in saints' lives and martyrologies, but this book will be concerned with the dialogues in prose, which have been particularly neglected as a group among scholars of late antiquity.

This situation is surprising, given the growth of interest both in the literary aspects of early Christian writing and in the important role played in late antiquity by rhetoric. After all, whether genuinely Platonic or not, such dialogues formed opinion, advocated key positions in the development of Christian thought, and were part of the process of "Christianization." Varied though they are, some certainly belong in any intellectual or philosophical history of late antiquity. But the actual number and range of surviving and known dialogues ought to make them an important subject of study in their own right. This short book, based on three lectures given at the Ruprecht-Karls-Universität Heidelberg in 2001,[1] and part of a larger project, aims simply to draw attention

---

[1] Averil Cameron, forthcoming c. I am very grateful to Prof. Andrea Jördens for her willingness to allow this revised English version.

to the extraordinary richness and importance of this material, and to set out some of the main questions it presents.

I confine myself here to late antiquity, and mainly to Christian writing in Greek. I do not of course mean to suggest an artificial divide. Latin dialogues are important; but many, including those by Augustine, have been well covered by others. In a recent conspicuous development in the scholarship on late antiquity, the interdependence of Greek and Syriac writing has been more and more clearly recognized, and this also extends to the writing of dialogues, with a further history in Arabic. I also believe that the *Adversus Iudaeos* literature—dialogues which claim to be between Christians and Jews—and its equivalent, the debates and dialogues between Christians and Muslims, need to be brought within studies of Christian dialogues in their entirety. Finally, as I argue in the Conclusion and will also contend elsewhere, it is artificial and misleading to separate Christian literature in late antiquity from the long history of dialogues and debates in Byzantium. This is not in order to posit an unrealistic continuity. Rather, certain trends in late antique dialogues, for instance the increasing influence of Aristotle, can be better understood if we do not merely follow this thread as far as Baghdad, through the educational system of the Syriac schools, but also extend our enquiry to the Byzantine centuries, where prose dialogue-writing also had an important and even more neglected history. It is perhaps more plausible to suggest something of a break in the continuity of written dialogues in the early medieval west,[2] but dialogues remained a favored way of writing for Christians in Byzantium, which constituted a literary form that was pursued in some periods with exceptional vigor.[3] This is one case where the conventional disciplinary boundaries between late antiquity and Byzantium can be seriously unhelpful.

I am grateful to my friends Greg Nagy and Scott Fitzgerald Johnson for their enthusiastic agreement to publish a revised version of the original English of the Haecker Lecture in the Hellenic Studies series, and to Yannis Papadogiannakis (again) for the original suggestion. Greg Nagy was (re)encountered in the context of the *Athens Dialogues* held by the Alexander S. Onassis Public Benefit Foundation in Athens in 2010, and it is also a pleasure to publish this book with the editorial encouragement of Scott Johnson, who was my doctoral student in Oxford and who shares my interest in later Greek literature. Some of what follows draws on work done by Alberto Rigolio in Oxford as research assistant in the context of a Leverhulme Emeritus Fellowship I held in the Faculty of Theology and Religion, 2011–2013. I am also grateful to my colleagues at Heidelberg for

---

[2]   Below, chapter 1.
[3]   Lucianic, satirical and verse dialogues were also important in Byzantium, and the line between these and the prose dialogues with which I am concerned can sometimes become blurred.

their invitation to give the Haecker Lecture, and for their hospitality and kindness in many other ways; particular thanks should go to Christian Witschel, Johannes Quack and Andrea Jördens. Many others have been extremely helpful as I began to see the range of issues surrounding the topic of dialogue, including Virginia Burrus, then President of the North American Patristics Society, for her invitation to speak at the annual North American Patristic Society conference in Chicago in May, 2009, Gillian Clark and the Directors of the Oxford Patristic Conference 2011, Volker Menze for his invitation to the Central European University, Budapest, Niels Gaul, also of the CEU, for stimulating exchanges about the "dialogic", Aziz al-Azmeh at the CEU, Margaret Mullett for her invitation to Dumbarton Oaks and for much else besides, Mossman Roueché and Richard Sorabji for answering my questions about Aristotle, Samuel N.C. Lieu for advice about Manichaeanism, Elodie Turquois, Ryan C. Fowler, and in Oxford especially Guy Stroumsa, Fergus Millar, Phil Booth and James Pettifer, sources of unfailing encouragement, generosity and advice. The picture of the baptistery at Nisibis which forms the frontispiece was taken while on a memorable visit to eastern Turkey with James Pettifer in September 2013, and I thank Elif Keser-Kayaalp for her invaluable help on this occasion. Alberto J. Quiroga Puertas read the entire text and Lucas Siorvanes of King's College London was enormously helpful at a much earlier stage in this work. Finally, my friend Elizabeth Clark of Duke University pioneered the application of literary theory to early Christian literature, and for this, as well as for our friendship, sustained over more than thirty years, she is owed my profound gratitude.

Oxford, July 2013

Introduction

THIS BOOK IS ABOUT A PARTICULAR FORM OF WRITING by Christians in late antiquity, sometimes referred to as "the philosophical dialogue"—although by no means all the dialogues in question can be regarded as philosophical. The subject is central to the much wider question of the development of a specifically Christian rhetoric, especially in Perelman's sense in which "the realm of rhetoric" constitutes "the entire universe of argumentative discourse,"[1] for Christian writers did indeed use the dialogue form as part of their argumentative endeavor.

Despite some promising signs of interest, these prose dialogues—literary discussions between two or more speakers on a specific question or group of related questions[2]—are still neglected as a significant component of late antique Christian literature. This is still more the case for Byzantium, even though dialogues continued to be written in Greek for many centuries and were particularly favored by Byzantine intellectuals in some periods. A very preliminary investigation conducted at an early stage in this research identified well over two hundred examples (taking a broad view of "dialogue") from the second century AD to the end of Byzantium. Some from the later period remain unpublished and many are still without modern critical editions or literary or rhetorical discussion. The actual total is likely to be much larger. Such dialogues have attracted scholars as a general phenomenon, especially in relation to the Renaissance, but such discussions rarely if ever include consideration of Greek dialogues from late antiquity, and still less those from the Byzantine period.[3] No doubt there are disciplinary and linguistic explanations for this omission, but as so often, it acts to prevent an overall and more complete analysis of what is in fact one

---

[1] Perelman 1982:x; cf. also Perelman and Olbrechts-Tyteca 1969.

[2] Cf. Hösle 2012:39, citing Isidore of Seville *Etymologies* 6.8.2, "a discussion between two or more persons which the Latins would call *sermo*"; 40, a "literary genre that primarily represents a conversation"; 45 (of philosophical dialogues), "a literary genre that represents a discussion of philosophical questions," going on to say that these will almost certainly be in prose, though verse is not absolutely excluded.

[3] The article "Dialogue" in Cancik and Schneider 2002:352–356 (K. H. Hölkeskamp) states that the dialogue form was more developed in the west than in Byzantium, and cites no Byzantine examples.

of the most enduring and fundamental of literary forms. I must mention here the comprehensive study by Vittorio Hösle, which deals with dialogues from Plato to the modern period. Hösle frequently mentions Methodius's *Symposium*, Gregory of Nyssa's *De Anima* and Augustine's Cassiciacum dialogues, and to a lesser extent Cicero and the *Octavius* of Minucius Felix, but his sketch of the history of dialogues[4] has little to say on late antiquity and nothing on Byzantium. Hösle's book is full of suggestive observations that can be usefully applied to the wider range of Greek Christian dialogues. But he writes as a philosopher concerned with philosophical argument and methodology, and furthermore, as an "objective idealist" concerned to reassert the importance of Platonism and Hegelianism. As he admits, his real subject is the history of western philosophy and its development since Descartes, in which he sees Christian dialogues, as inter-religious dialogues, as no more than a "sub-genre." Hösle's book is important in its own terms, but the quantity and variety of the material to which I draw attention here suggests the need for a different evaluation.

The written dialogues with which I am concerned purport to be, and sometimes are, accounts of conversations.[5] They may contain narrative elements, but they may also present themselves like dramatic scripts, as if they have been or will be performed. This is a subject which needs further treatment elsewhere. They easily fall into the three types thought since antiquity to be characteristic of Platonic dialogues: the dramatic, that is, the conversation itself; the narrative, reporting a conversation; and the mixed, where an initial direct dialogue then reports a previous conversation.[6] We know rather little about how they were heard and received in late antiquity, in comparison with the social performance of rhetoric in late Byzantium,[7] but they were certainly intended to persuade. Some, at least, seem closer to orality than many other sorts of late antique literature, and others claim to be verbatim records of actual debates.[8] Chapter two will consider evidence of such actual debates from late antiquity, and it is not surprising to find the question of whether or not the debate in question "really" took place occupying a prominent place in the existing literature, though it is not always the most appropriate question to ask. It is also a difficult one, in the absence of independent evidence, especially as many Christian dialogues adopt a fiction of orality, by introducing elements of verisimilitude designed to persuade the reader that he or she is indeed reading about a real

---

[4] Hösle 2012:71–119.
[5] See Hösle 2012:19–47 "Conversation and Dialogue."
[6] Diogenes Laertius, 3.50; see Döring 2011:25.
[7] See Grünbart 2007; Mullett 1984 (2001).
[8] Below, chapter 2. The question of orality features in scholarship on the Platonic dialogues, but like so much else remains to be studied in relation to the dialogues I am dealing with.

discussion. Sometimes these elements derive from Platonic models, especially the *Republic* and the *Symposium*, in an exercise of imitation, or rather of intertextuality.[9] In general, though with some exceptions, the Platonizing elements are literary/rhetorical rather than philosophical.[10] Indeed a further question that emerges from considering Christian dialogues as a group is the increasing resort to Aristotelian logic, which was later to become more and more important both in Greek and Syriac Christian-Muslim debates and in Byzantium. The influence of Aristotle is strongly felt in many later Byzantine theological dialogues, some of which, despite many protestations against syllogistic and against the dependence on Aristotle, were accompanied by long lists of syllogisms;[11] but it was also already apparent in late antiquity.[12]

A letter by Basil of Caesarea lets us see the extent to which Plato was valued for his literary genius. Writing to Diodorus, then a presbyter in Antioch but later bishop of Tarsus, he describes two works sent to him by the latter, both of which seem to have been in dialogue form (neither has survived).[13] He prefers the second for its "simple and natural style," whereas the first "is much more elaborately adorned with rich diction, [and] many features and niceties of dialogue," which "require considerable time to read, and much mental labor both to gather its meaning and retain it in the memory." He also disapproves of the "abuse of our opponents and the support of our own side, which are thrown in, although they may seem to add some charms of dialectic to the treatise," and which "break the continuity of the thought and weaken the strength of the argument by causing interruption and delay." Basil continues in an interesting way:

> I know that your intelligence is perfectly well aware that the heathen philosophers who wrote dialogues, Aristotle and Theophrastus, went straight to the point, because they were aware of not being gifted with the graces of Plato. Plato on the other hand, with his great power of writing, at the same time attacks opinions and incidentally makes fun of his characters, assailing now the rashness and recklessness of a Thrasymachus, the levity and frivolity of a Hippias, and the arrogance and pomposity of a Protagoras. When, however, he introduces

---

9   For the heuristic value (or lack thereof) of these terms, see the papers in Rhoby and Schiffer 2010, especially Mullett 2010 and Nilsson 2010.

10 "Stylistic" might be a better term. I cannot deal here with the contention that the use made of Plato by the Christian apologists, including Theodoret, was rhetorical rather than philosophical (Siniossoglou 2008:21–27; see chapter 3 below).

11 Below, chapter 3.

12 I hope to treat these issues and the Byzantine dialogues elsewhere.

13 *Letter* 135, Courtonne 1961:49–51; see also *Letter* 348, a reference I owe to Alberto J. Quiroga Puertas.

unmarked characters into his dialogues, he uses the interlocutors for making the point clear, but does not admit anything more belonging to the characters into the argument. An instance of this is in the Laws.

Translation NPNF VIII, 200–201

Over and above their theological content Christian dialogues raise questions of literarity and intertextuality. Yet while no one can now question the centrality of rhetoric in late antique education and culture, the works of the rhetorical writers do not lay down rules for dialogue. No rhetorical treatise focuses directly on dialogue, or on oral debate for that matter, and the Socratic background to later dialogues included a traditional opposition between rhetoric and the Socratic discourse.[14] A few hints from the second century onwards suggest that dialogue was thought of as being different from rhetoric, as being less formal and more conversational.[15] In Lucian's dialogue known as the "Twice-accused" or "Double Indictment" (*Bis accusatus*), Rhetoric complains that he has deserted her for dialogue:

> He [Lucian] assumed a haughty air, and neglected, nay, utterly abandoned me; having conceived a violent affection for the bearded old person yonder, whom you may know from his dress to be Dialogue, and who passes for a son of Philosophy"... He [Lucian] is not ashamed to "submit himself to the comedian's fetters of bald question and answer. He, whose thoughts should have found utterance in thundering oratory, is content to weave a puny network of conversation. [16]

Loeb translation

The defense put forward by the "Syrian," i.e. Lucian, is that rhetoric had become corrupted with over-embellishment, and that he had therefore decided to retire from the hurly-burly of the law-courts "to the walks of the Academy or the Lyceum, there to enjoy, in the delightful society of Dialogue, that tranquil discourse which aims not at noisy acclamations."[17]

"Dialogue" in return, attempting, according to Lucian, rhetorical discourse, and lacking skill or experience, instead of the "conversational style to which I am accustomed,"[18] promptly complains that Lucian has lowered the level

---

[14] The opposition can however be deceptive, as argued by L. Rossetti: see chapter 1 below.
[15] See Pernot 1993a:421–434; the *rendez-vous* that Pernot claims failed to take place is that between dialogue and rhetoric.
[16] Lucian *Double Indictment*, 28.
[17] Lucian *Double Indictment*, 32.
[18] Lucian *Double Indictment*, 33.

of dialogue from the heights of philosophy to that of comedy and burlesque. Lucian replies, the jury votes and Lucian is acquitted.

If dialogue as such was not taught in the rhetorical schools, this was not true of argument, and attention has been drawn to the prominence of Hermogenes's treatise *On Issues*, the subject of a commentary by Menander Rhetor.[19] Many of the writers of Greek dialogues in late antiquity had received an excellent rhetorical training and the dialogues they produced might well seem to qualify as part of what has been called the "Third Sophistic," a term sometimes applied to the extraordinary flowering of Christian rhetoric in late antiquity.[20] Despite the lack of direct rhetorical precepts for such works, they surely belong at least in the wider sense (and in some cases more specifically) to the history of rhetoric, the art of persuasion, in late antiquity. The dialogues considered here range more widely than the technical realm of rhetoric (though some are highly rhetorical), just as they range more widely than the philosophical; but in the broader sense they all qualify as an important part of the rhetorical formation of Christian thought and Christian discourse.[21]

Dialogues rarely feature as such in general works on Christian literature.[22] Setting out the material and its potential is the first step towards a better understanding of the many issues and questions that it raises, and providing such an introduction is my aim in the chapters that follow. I agree wholeheartedly with a recent contributor to *Antiquité tardive* who remarks that we still lack an analysis of late antique Christian writing that would do justice to its social dynamism and intellectual and literary force.[23] These dialogues are part of that story.

---

[19] Heath 2004, especially chapter 7. Hermogenes's treatise set out model arguments in "quasi-dialogue form" (Heath 2004: chap. 9). Katos 2011 offers an interpretation of Palladius's *Dialogue on the Life of John Chrysostom* in this light, and see Katos 2007, with Gronewald 1991 (I owe the last reference to Scott Johnson); date and circumstances: Van Nuffelen 2013.

[20] Schamp 2006, who begins his discussion of the birth of Christian rhetoric with Justin's *Dialogue with Trypho*, on which see below, chapter 1. For the idea of a Third Sophistic, Pernot 1993b:1.14n9, though the term is proving controversial and the range of authors included varies considerably: Averil Cameron, forthcoming a, and see Penella 2013.

[21] An accessible overview of rhetorical training in late antiquity and Byzantium can be found in Mary Whitby 2010. A recent collection dealing with aspects of rhetoric in late antiquity is Quiroga Puertas 2013.

[22] An exception is Moreschini and Norelli 2005:2.15–16, 579, and see also Weber 2000.

[23] Van Hoof 2010, and see also Formisano 2007.

1

Did Christians "Do Dialogue"?

THE ATTRACTION OF PLATO was felt powerfully in late antiquity, and is still felt today. As one illustration, the novelist Iris Murdoch was also a teacher of philosophy in Oxford, and deeply interested in Plato.[1] She even composed two Platonic dialogues, on the themes of art and religion, in which she introduced the figure of the young Plato as a speaker and dramatic persona;[2] Plato plays the role of Alcibiades in the *Symposium*. In the author's note, she explains that these dialogues were meant to be performed, "either in modern dress or in period costume," and the published version notes such a performance of the first of them, *Art and Eros*, which had taken place at the National Theatre in London in February, 1980, directed by Michael Kustow (to whom the published version is dedicated). The very concept of dialogues as performative at once raises questions about their interpretation and whether they have a single meaning. These are questions, including that of authorship and intention, which are central to the focus that Hösle places on intersubjectivity.[3]

In the late fourth century, soon after the death of his brother Basil, Gregory of Nyssa composed a dialogue on the soul, with himself and his dying sister Macrina as the interlocutors.[4] Gregory's *Life of Macrina* is one of the classics of late antique Christian literature, and Macrina's role as teacher, the Christian version of Diotima/Socrates in Plato's *Symposium*, has long been noted.[5] The *Life* is a highly complex and artful text, even if Gregory presents it as deliberately "simple." Similarly, Gregory's use of the dialogue form in *On the Soul* is clearly a deliberate literary choice, carefully adopting a Platonic model.[6] This literary choice allows Gregory to make a dramatic play by attributing a rejection of dialectic to Macrina, who is given the role of a Christian Diotima, but who in the

---

[1] See Murdoch 1977.
[2] Murdoch 1986.
[3] Hösle 2012, e.g. 11 for "a genre of intersubjectivity."
[4] Gregory of Nyssa *On the Soul and On Resurrection*, translation in Roth 1993.
[5] On the *Life*, see Krueger 2000.
[6] See Wessel 2010; Williams 1993; Burrus 2000; Hösle 2012:136, 397–398.

Christian context of late antiquity remains a woman educated at home by her mother only in the Scriptures and the Psalms; this contrasted sharply of course with her brothers Gregory and Basil, who had been given the best education available in literary *paideia*. *On the Soul*, this most Platonic of Christian dialogues, undercuts its own philosophical framework and uses the dialogue form to express the tension between Christian faith and philosophical reasoning. We need not suppose that such a dialogue "really happened" (though the temptation to read the *Life of Macrina* as a real portrait has been strong, especially among those interested in women in late antiquity). For Gregory, the figure of Macrina is a literary trope.[7] Yet she was also his real sister and he used her in his literary treatments to work out ideas of his own, thereby beautifully exemplifying the ambiguities and ambivalence inherent in the dialogue form.

A very large number of dialogues survive from late antiquity and the Byzantine period, and Gregory of Nyssa's *On the Soul* is hardly typical. Yet as we have seen, it raises some of the key issues that surround this form of Christian writing. My subject, and the titles of the three chapters published here, are indebted to a provocative collection of essays edited by Simon Goldhill in 2009 with the title *The End of Dialogue in Antiquity*.[8] Goldhill's introduction is entitled "Why don't Christians do dialogue?" His broad argument is that open debate ended with the success of Christianization: Christians debated, but they could not "dialogue" in the Socratic sense of conducting open-ended discussion. The end was always a foregone conclusion; thus what may seem to be dialogues do not represent genuine dialogue or debate, but something much more sinister, an artificial genre or an authoritarian discourse leading not to the opening of debate but rather to its closing down. Goldhill thus identifies "dialogue" with freedom, and with democracy, and his model is the supposedly open-ended Socratic dialogue.

It is not new to argue that the dialogue form that began in classical Greece ended with the rise of Christianity. We find the idea inherent, for instance, in the standard work on the classical dialogue by Rudolf Hirzel, published in 1895,[9] though Hirzel devotes little actual space to considering the Christian, or indeed the late antique, period. Goldhill's argument ignores the later history of

---

[7] See E. A. Clark 1998:426.

[8] Goldhill 2009; some elements of the argument presented here were first aired in a paper at the annual conference of the North American Patristic Society in Chicago in 2010. P. Van Nuffelen 2014 also discusses Goldhill and Lim, but comes to different conclusions. I am grateful to Peter Van Nuffelen for sharing his paper with me.

[9] See Hirzel 1895: vol. 2, chap. 7; for Christian dialogue, see Bardy 1957, classifying Christian dialogues as either apologetic, theological, biographical or Scriptural; Hoffmann 1966; Voss 1970; P. F. Beatrice 1983. For Hirzel as the originator of the idea that dialogue ended with the advent of Christianity, see Lim 2009:151.

dialogues, and by implication denigrates Byzantium in relation to the history of western culture. But there are several other strands within it, in particular the claim that Christian discussion could not be "real" discussion, because it aimed by definition at proving an authoritarian position—orthodoxy, which was not to be questioned. I confess to seeming to give some encouragement to such a view in 1986 when delivering the Sather Lectures at Berkeley, when I spoke of a "totalizing discourse" as having been at least partly achieved by the sixth century, a time when the aim of church and state alike was certainly to establish a settlement and arrive at a uniform ideology.[10] That phrase, used in a study of the development of Christian rhetorical expression in late antiquity, has been taken up by others, perhaps too often.[11] I followed it up with a paper that tried to apply an ascetic model to early Byzantine society,[12] and indeed a closing-in of horizons is a popular way of looking at the early Byzantine period.[13] Several emperors—Zeno, Heraclius—resorted to forbidding any further discussion of religious matters and ordering silence.[14] They were following the precedent set by the earlier impatience with dialectic famously expressed by Constantine when he first heard of the Christian disputes in Egypt surrounding Arius.[15] If this characterization of Byzantium is correct, the historical implications are profound; but in fact I argue elsewhere that it is not.[16] Byzantium was very far from being the closed society that its own Orthodox self-representation tends to suggest. "Orthodox" and official doctrines were very often questioned, while the rhetorical skill evinced in the production of dialogues, among a wide range of other works, was a pathway by which those not already belonging to the elite could obtain secular or ecclesiastical advancement, making Byzantium a far more open society than is supposed. Those who believe in the standard image have been taken in by the smooth surface of the Byzantines' own rhetoric. In contrast I want to argue even more strongly than I did in 1995 that contrary to the idea that discussion was "shut down" in the fifth or sixth century, what happened was the very opposite. I quote from that paper of 1995: "the constant and public search for certainty," for orthodoxy in contrast to heresy, "generated

---

[10] Averil Cameron 1991b, chap. 6; cf. Averil Cameron 2012.

[11] Some questions: De Bruyn 1993, arguing for the limits of rhetoric. Markus 2009 argues for closure in the late sixth century, though focusing on the west, while also remarking that "ends are new beginnings" (p. 13).

[12] Averil Cameron 1995.

[13] As also implied in Athanassiadi 2010.

[14] See Lim 1995a:227.

[15] Eusebius *Life of Constantine* 2.69; Socrates *Ecclesiastical History* 2.7. For distrust of dialectic and disapproval of Christian dispute and argument expressed by Christians including the ecclesiastical historian Socrates, see Lim 1995b:215–226.

[16] Averil Cameron 2008a; Averil Cameron, forthcoming a.

its own resistance."[17] "Instead of calming and stabilizing society, the much vaunted serenity of the Christian emperors ... in actuality stimulated division." The greater the effort to control and enforce, the more resistance showed itself. The settled religious establishment was desired and boasted about,[18] but never achieved in practice. Late antique historians have learned to be very skeptical of claims made in official language, especially in the case of legal evidence, and the same skepticism needs to be applied to religious rhetoric. The reality was continual struggle, reinvention and resistance, above all, continual talk and continual arguing; not only was Christian orthodoxy not settled in the sixth century or in any other named period: the process of trying to achieve it required constant and energetic efforts in the direction of legal and other kinds of enforcement.[19]

This is far from suggesting that genuine dialogue stopped with Christianization, unless one simply rules out as irrelevant all the mass of material about religious debate which we find continuing right through the Byzantine period until the very end. This is indeed just what Goldhill does. His kind of dialogue is an elite form of polite open-minded conversation between educated people. He not only denies the relevance of such genres as Christian "catechism" or questions and answers (let alone conciliar arguments), but also the actual dialogues and disputations that survive in huge numbers.[20] They include not only dialogues between Christians and Jews, or Christians and Muslims, but also, for instance, a reported debate between Maximus Confessor and the patriarch Pyrrhus in Carthage in the 640s, and many, many more.[21]

A first theme, therefore, hinges on the question of whether Christians really did stop "dialoguing" (and if so what that means for the nature of the late antique and Byzantine world). Goldhill's contention is taken up in a paper in the same volume by Daniel Boyarin, who applies just such an idea of an "epistemic shift" in the fifth century to explain otherwise puzzling features in the Talmuds.[22] Both Goldhill and Boyarin derive support from the important book by Richard Lim on public debate in late antiquity.[23] While Lim memorably

---

17 Averil Cameron 1995:157.

18 For stress laid by Christians on social *homonoia* in the pre-Constantinian period, see Lim 1995b:206–208; emphasis on deference (*sunkatabasis*) and unanimity (*sundiathesis*): Eusebius *Ecclesiastical History* 7.24.7–8.

19 See Averil Cameron 2007.

20 For some examples, see Averil Cameron 1991a; however Byzantine dialogue literature has never been studied in its totality.

21 PG 91:288–353; below, chapter 2.

22 Boyarin 2009a.

23 Lim 1995a; see also Lim 1999 (where I read "triumph" as "triumphalism," and the methods to which Christians resorted to achieve dominance); Lim 1995b; for "social closure," see Lim 1995a:104–105, 106, though compare Lim 2009:153–156, on the classical symposium as an elite

argues for "the containment of the *Logos*," his work in fact brings the actual extent of public debating in late antiquity vividly to our attention, not least between Christians and Manichaeans. Nevertheless, he argues that from the fifth century AD onwards, public debates were "no more than show cases."[24] Following Lim, Daniel Boyarin maintains that there was in that period a loss of faith in rational argument, constituting "an emergency in discourse."[25] Both Lim and Boyarin detect a move towards an authoritarian stance (which Boyarin calls "hierarchisation"), exemplified by the increasing use of lists, florilegia and systematization, and Lim implies that "religious competitors" were "bound by the parameters of these norms [he is here referring to conciliar precedents] when they engaged in controversy."[26] Lim sees this shift as happening in the fifth century, and connects it with what he also sees as a lack of actual discussion in church councils. The modes of argument employed in church councils do indeed call for more discussion than they have so far received. Meanwhile, chapter 2 below will consider possible reasons for what I prefer to call increasing technologization, and take issue with the idea expressed by Lim and Boyarin that debates were reduced to silence.

Christian debates were not entirely one way. Maijastina Kahlos, for instance, has argued in relation to the late fourth and early fifth centuries that both Christians and pagans at times tried to find middle ground, for instance when they debated on matters of monotheism and polytheism.[27] Apologetic was another type of writing, which, it would seem, could not by its nature be wholly one-sided.[28] There was no single formula for Christian discussion. But Christians certainly did often tend towards the authoritarian; in that sense they were not open-minded, and of course the very project of conversion implies that the convert has been convinced and is willing to separate himself from his previous convictions.[29] The processes of Christianization, and the identification and targeting of error demanded mechanisms of separation and the delineation of borderlines.[30]

---

form of conviviality. Asking why Christians did not do this kind of dialogue is for several reasons the wrong question; in practice, "Christians 'dialogued' as never before" (Lim 2009:171).

[24] Lim 1995a:106.

[25] Boyarin 2009a:224.

[26] Lim 1995a:226.

[27] Kahlos 2007:141–153; see also G. Clark 2009:133: however, compare Humfress 2012, with a list of Augustine's controversialist works at 324–325; Führer 2012, in the same volume, argues from a broader definition of dialogue in Augustine's writings to its continuation throughout his life: Augustine went on "being dialectical" and many of his writings sprang from a "dialectical mindset" (valuable general remarks on the nature of dialogue, 274–279).

[28] Kahlos 2007:79–80, but see further below.

[29] Kahlos 2007:78, 83–84.

[30] See Averil Cameron 2008a.

In practice Christians in late antiquity (and in Byzantium, for that matter), were constantly "dialoguing," engaging in actual and written debates, arguments and disputations. The question is what form these debates took. Were they open-ended, as Goldhill requires, or were they, as he imagines in contrast, more usually polemical, apologetic or even encyclopedic? My wider project is to study the large corpus of known and surviving dialogues in both late antiquity and the Byzantine period, particularly, but not only, from the literary point of view. How did dialogues relate to other forms of Christian writing, and what techniques did they use? How did they relate to actual debates,[31] and did the latter—as well as the rest of the large body of Christian writing, which had its own effect—conduce to social harmony, or conversely, to division and even violence?[32] What if anything can they tell us about religious communication in the Roman empire?

Another recent survey, indeed, has seen disputation as a key mode of inter-religious communication in antiquity.[33] But in order to begin to answer any of these many interlocking questions it is necessary to draw up a comprehensive list of all the many known and surviving dialogues, not to mention those embedded in other kinds of works. Meanwhile chapter 3 below will outline some of the issues surrounding the literary form—or forms—of the dialogue, while chapter 2 will set the scene for such a discussion by considering the evidence for actual argument, debate, and dialogue in late antiquity.

In the rest of this chapter, I want to return to the relation of Christian dialogues to classical ones, and to survey the many different kinds of dialogic material that would need to be covered in a full study of this neglected field.

Whether Socratic dialogues were as open-ended and "democratic" as Goldhill contends, seems doubtful. In Plato's dialogues, Socrates' affected ignorance may lead to an *aporia*, lack of resolution, but his questions are often leading, and in the later dialogues at least, Plato gives up the pretense and allows Socrates to be the mouthpiece for theoretical discourses, or even to be the listener while another character expresses philosophical argument at some length. The nature of the Socratic *elenchos* remains a matter of considerable disagreement. The very nature of dialectics can be seen in terms of competition; as one scholar puts it, "Greek dialectical encounters, like Greek erotic encounters, involved the constant negotiation of who was on top and who on bottom," amounting to a "dynamic interplay of balance" in which "the invitee has to risk his pride and any general sense of superiority that he may have to engage in

---

[31] Here I part company with Lim 2009, who advocates "decoupling" them from attitudes to intellectual conformity, and seeing them as a "boutique literary form."

[32] See Lim 1995b.

[33] See Cancik 2008.

the dialectic."[34] Leaving aside the insoluble "Socratic problem," interpretation of Plato has veered between the opposing poles of doctrinal and historical or dialogic approaches.[35] In a long series of articles Livio Rossetti has pointed to the rhetorical nature of Socrates's arguments and strategies, even when he famously seems to condemn rhetoric as such.[36] In other words, Socratic dialogues are not what they may seem, and Plato's dialogues are only one subset, albeit a famous and important one, of the known corpus of some two hundred Socratic dialogues. As for our present question, which relates to dialogues in late antiquity, Daniel Boyarin provocatively argues that Platonic dialogues themselves were mono-logic—the opposite of open-ended.[37] Moreover, late antique dialogue-writers had other precedents besides Plato, and even when they did imitate Plato they were drawn most to a limited number of Platonic dialogues—in particular, the *Symposium*, book 1 of the *Republic*, *Phaedo*, *Phaedrus*, and the *Protagoras*, useful for dramatic and narrative settings and for the subject matter.[38] Furthermore, in later periods Aristotle and Aristotelian dialectic were stronger influences than Plato on many Christian dialogues and debates. This is especially true for the Byzantine period, as I hope to show elsewhere.

Another way of looking at classical dialogues has been in the context of sympotic or symposiastic literature.[39] While some Christian writers were drawn to this mode, they are not my focus of attention here. At the beginning of the fourth century Methodius of Olympus did indeed present the Christian theme of asceticism and virginity in the guise of a symposium; I will return in chapter 3 to this curious work and to Methodius's other dialogues. My main concern here is with Christian dialogues in Greek, though Christians, not least Augustine himself, also wrote dialogues in Latin.[40] But it is hard to see many Christian dialogues as being similar either to the talk at classical Greek symposia or to the literary conversations of an Athenaeus or a Macrobius.[41] Nevertheless there

---

34 Lane 2011:253.
35 See Hart and Tejera 1997, a collection not without its faults but offering a useful introduction to the issues; see in particular Rossetti 1997 and Smith 1997, both of which raise questions of orality and performativity which can also be asked of Christian dialogues.
36 Including for example Rossetti 1989, 2007, 2011.
37 Boyarin 2009b.
38 Hösle 2012, part two, includes a detailed discussion of the subtleties of structure and content in Plato's dialogues, and see below and chapter 3 on Methodius. Except for the *Republic* 1 and the *Protagoras*, those to which allusions are most often made in our texts are not the so-called Socratic dialogues.
39 König 2009 (Clement, Athenaeus, Methodius, Macrobius), 2012; see Martin 1931, and for the social and material context Murray 1995; also Smith 2003.
40 Schmidt 1977; G. Clark 2009; Stock 2010, and see chapter 2 below.
41 For Athenaeus, see now Jacob 2013 and for Macrobius, and for much general discussion, see Goldlust 2010.

are surely connections still to be explored with both of these, and between the sympotic works of Plutarch and the types of dialogue written by Christians.[42] Lucian's extensive output also needs examination from this point of view, even if his influence seems to have been felt later by Byzantine *littérateurs* and authors of "satirical" dialogues more than by late antique or Byzantine philosophical or theological dialogue-writers.[43] As Richard Miles has pointed out, and before him Jacques Fontaine,[44] Christian dialogue was pursued in earnest; its aim was not clever or diverting conversation, but truth.

Debate is inherent in the New Testament writings; the disciples of Jesus asked themselves what his life and teaching meant while he was alive, and still more after his death, and Paul continually exhorts the new communities to distance themselves from error.[45] Justin's *Dialogue with Trypho*, from the first half of the second century, is the earliest example of what was to become a major Christian group of dialogues, commonly known as the *Adversus Iudaeos* literature, and designed to demonstrate the superiority of Christianity over Judaism.[46] Much has been written about Justin's work, whose two contrasting sections make it something of a hybrid, if indeed they are not two separate works or a dossier; it cannot be denied, however, that it already exemplifies what Tessa Rajak has called "talking *at*," and Elizabeth Clark "talking back,"[47] that is, the desire to win an argument. In the late second century, the teaching of Bardesanes of Edessa was also expressed in Syriac in the form of a dialogue between Bardesanes and the astrologer Awida, apparently by one of his disciples.[48] Dialogue was to be a major type of literary production in Syriac in later centuries,[49] and Bardesanes himself is credited with dialogues composed against the Marcionites,[50] but as Han Drijvers pointed out, the *Book of the Laws of Countries*

---

[42] See Kechagia 2011; Oikonomopoulou 2011; König 2007. Eshleman 2012 links pagan and Christian writing in the early empire, a welcome—because still unusual—feature among studies of the Second Sophistic period. The relevance of the latter to early Christian dialogues has yet to be fully explored.

[43] This may well be a somewhat artificial distinction, which fails to do justice to Lucian's own engagement with Plato.

[44] Miles 2009:148; Fontaine 1968; 1988:62.

[45] Cf. Edwards 2009:2, "there is hardly any book of our New Testament that does not contain an invective against false teaching"; see also Averil Cameron and R. G. Hoyland 2011: Introduction.

[46] Rajak 1999:59–80. For Christian writing from the first to the fifth centuries, see Young et al. 2004. Anti-Jewish dialogues (*Adversus Iudaeos* texts): Schreckenberg 1999; Külzer 1999; Lahey 2007; Frederiksen and Irshai 2008.

[47] See E. A. Clark 1999:128–132.

[48] Drijvers 1994 (anti-Marcionite and to be identified with the dialogue on fate translated into Greek and known to Eusebius and Epiphanius); Drijvers 2006; Ramelli 2009a, 2009b:1–28.

[49] A good starting point for the links between Greek and Syriac is provided by Watt 2010 and see Johnson, forthcoming, and Tannous 2013.

[50] Eusebius *Ecclesiastical History* 4.30; Watt 2010:V.

is not really dialogic, being much more a vehicle for Bardesanes's own views on fate and free will.[51] Nor, despite its nod to Plato's *Republic* in the opening passage, is it in fact Socratic.[52] Bardesanes is made to say 'It is teachers who are questioned, but they themselves do not put questions. And if they do (it is) to lead the ideas of the one who is questioned upon the right track, so that he may put good questions and they may understand his meaning. For it is an excellent thing that a man knows how to formulate questions.'[53] Bardesanes holds forth on fate and free will, and the nature of the heavenly bodies, all topics destined to be treated often in later centuries. The *Book of the Laws of Countries* also differs from the Greek examples from the second century in being more philosophical, with clear debts to the *Timaeus*, and to Middle Platonism and Stoicism (Drijvers refers to its "artificial character"). Dialogue also appears in the form of disputes between Paul and Simon Magus in the Ps. Clementine literature,[54] to which the *Book of the Laws of Countries* is somehow related, and signals the start of a literary form which was to become very important and very central in Syriac literature.

It is true that in its very genesis, Christian dialogue was controversialist; Justin's aim, like that of other second-century Christian writers such as Tatian and the Latin writer Tertullian, was from the start to argue against pagans, Jews and heretical Christians. Justin wrote against heretics, Tatian against "Greeks," i.e. pagans.[55] A little later, Tertullian produced an extensive *oeuvre* consisting of treatises and writings with pagans, heterodox Christians and Jews as their targets. Assuming its authenticity, the opening of his treatise against the Jews is interesting from our point of view: the treatise is presented as a written exposition, on the basis of written records, of an actual debate between a Christian and a Jewish proselyte, which had turned into an unruly shouting match:

> It happened very recently that a debate was held between a Christian and a proselyte Jew. Through the tug-of-war exchange between them, they dragged the day into evening. Also, through the clamouring from some supporters of both individuals, the truth was being obscured as if by a cloud. Therefore, as a full explanation was impossible on account of everyone speaking at once, it was decided to settle the questions

---

[51] For some of the issues surrounding the text, originally written in Syriac and very soon translated into Greek, after which it became widely known, see Drijvers 1966, especially 67, 75–76. Bardesanes' cosmology: Drijvers 1966:96–126.

[52] Bowersock 1990:32.

[53] Bowersock 1990:7.

[54] See Côté 2001a, 2001b.

[55] For the genesis of Christian controversialist writing in the early centuries, see Inglebert 2001:395–400; Le Boulluec 1985.

that have been raised in writing, after a more careful examination of the texts.[56]

The texts in question are the Jewish Scriptures, and we have here already a dialogue whose argument is based on proof texts and their interpretation. It immediately raises many questions, for instance about the extent, if any, of actual debate between Jews and Christians at Carthage, where there was certainly a Jewish community, and about the nature of Judaism at the time.[57] It is clear enough that what follows, even at this early date, is a polemic, not a dialogue. It seems, then, as though the birth of Christian literary dialogues in Greek was connected to Christian polemic against Jews and to Christian arguments against heresy.

In general, indeed, we can say that dialogue was one of the literary modes in which the vast literature aimed at establishing Christian superiority was expressed. Its origins cannot be separated from the polemical or controversialist urge; dialogues were part of the effort to establish orthodoxy, especially if orthodoxy is understood in the broad sense set out by Hervé Inglebert in his important work on the development of a comprehensive Christian system of knowledge.[58]

This is not the place to rehearse the issues of conceptualization and methodology surrounding the concept of orthodoxy, which have given rise to so much writing in recent years.[59] Suffice it here to say that there was no simple chronological development towards a single orthodoxy. In its absence we can place emphasis on different aspects, on process, or on anthropological and sociological approaches. But one desideratum remains: we need a full analysis of the kinds of texts through which contemporaries struggled (again and again) to establish their own sense of what was and was not right belief ("orthodoxy") and to demonstrate the falsity of other versions. These texts include dialogues.

Yet perhaps it is not so straightforward. The anti-Jewish dialogues, in particular, are often dismissed as stereotypes, with one end only, to show Christian superiority and if possible the inevitable conversion of the Jewish interlocutors. But not all dialogues are so clear-cut. Dialogue, after all, involves more than one interlocutor. Might we see even in this genre of Christian dialogues an exemplar of the Bakhtinian concept of the "dialogic," with an inherent open-endedness, albeit different from that attributed by Goldhill to the Socratic dialogues?[60]

---

[56] Translation, Dunn 2004:68–69; see Dunn also for the authenticity of the work.
[57] See the brief remarks of Dunn 2004:47–51.
[58] Inglebert 2001:413–461.
[59] See for orientation Le Boulluec 2000; Ayres 2006; also Averil Cameron 2012 (2013).
[60] Bakhtin 1981, and see the classic discussion of Bakhtin and the dialogic in Kristeva 1981:64–91.

Bakhtin's concept of *heteroglossia* implies potential fluidity of meaning, a postmodernist shifting instability, and it is at least worth asking the question of whether this might help towards a better reading of some of these early Christian texts.[61] Writing on Gregory of Nyssa, Susan Wessel argues that Gregory's choice of the dialogue form for his *On the Soul* allows "for the possibility of interpreting seemingly contradictory ideas in an integrated fashion."[62] The paradox is that Macrina's alleged hostility to dialectic is framed in a literary production which adopts the trappings of Greek philosophy; similarly, Justin's seemingly shrill *Dialogue with Trypho* begins with a clear evocation of Platonic dialogic scene-setting.[63] The latter's opening sets a classical scene of civilized encounter and conversation in the portico of a gymnasium, in Platonic fashion,[64] while in a narrative within a narrative Justin relates his own conversion from philosophy (latterly Platonism) to Christianity, after which he maintains that in Christian argument philosophers must yield to the prophets. In what later became a trope, Trypho's companions laugh at Justin (8.3, 9.2), but Trypho himself is not converted (another later trope), and looks forward to further discussion "to continue our study of the Scriptures" (143.1).[65]

A more dialogic reading might help in the context of the current preoccupation among scholars of late antiquity and early Christianity with identity and self-definition.[66] Indeed, Andrew Jacobs has applied such a reading to the *Dialogue with Trypho*, arguing that it is in fact susceptible of a more nuanced interpretation that can help us to get beyond the obstacles put in our way by the Christian authors themselves.[67] "To read such texts dialogically, in a Bakhtinian sense, is to refuse the absolute separation of self and other that ancient Christians anxiously demand."[68] Jacobs is not offering a literary reading for its

---

[61] Also on Bakhtin, see E. A. Clark 1999:122–124, with bibliography. Rossetti 1997 also offers useful suggestions for the analysis of Christian dialogues.

[62] Wessel 2010:380n47.

[63] Ed. Bobichon 2003; Minns and Parvis 2009, and see Munnich 2012 (a dossier); the opening evokes Xenophon *Memorabilia* 1.1.10 as well as Plato.

[64] The dialogue is set in Ephesus according to Eusebius *Ecclesiastical History* 4.18, who also calls it a dialogue *against* the Jews, one among many apologetic and polemical works he lists as being by Justin. For continuing Platonic elements in the rest of the dialogue, and traces of the *Phaedrus*, *Timaeus*, and *Protagoras*, see Hoffmann 1996:16–17. Rajak, who wants to see the dialogue as foundational in the history of Christian anti-Jewish hostility, calls it "a conscious contribution to a new Christian literature" (Rajak 1999:80; see 65–66 for Justin's philosophical culture and 66–67 for the context in Justin's other writings); also Edwards 1991. Analysis of the dramatic locations in many dialogues, especially Plato's: Hösle 2012:210–236.

[65] Against Rajak, see Horner 1999.

[66] See for instance many works by Judith Lieu, especially J. Lieu 1996, 2002a, 2002b, 2004.

[67] Jacobs 2007; for reactions to Rajak's reading of the *Dialogue with Trypho*, see Jacobs 2007:296n18, and for Bakhtin, Jacobs 2007:293–295.

[68] Jacobs 2007:295.

own sake. Nor is he trying in any simple way to "recover" an actual rapprochement between early Christianity and Judaism.[69] Nevertheless he writes from the perspective of a historian of Jews in the Roman empire, and he is therefore also exercised by the problem of literal as well as figurative encounters with Jews on the part of Christians in the first Christian centuries.[70] In other words, Jacobs too is concerned at heart with the question of what relation there is, if any, between the dialogue texts and social reality, a question that keeps asserting itself as we look further into these Christian dialogues. As Jacobs observes,[71] this search, with the question of whether the debates were "real," and whether the texts can tell us about "real" conditions, has been a primary aim in previous scholarship. When so many of the texts themselves are just that—texts, without direct evidence of their audience or circumstances—this is indeed difficult to establish. If it is a real question at all, it is surely one for the stage when we have a much more complete and comprehensive understanding of all the dialogue material, not just of isolated examples or parts of the whole which happen, like the anti-Jewish dialogues, to interest a particular constituency of scholars and thus to have been more studied than the rest.

While I accept that Christian writing, including dialogues, was inherently designed to convince (to that extent agreeing with Goldhill),[72] a more dialogic reading of specific texts may nevertheless represent a salutary step in the search for a less simplistic view of a huge and varied range of material, and in particular, help to avoid the ever-present temptation of reading off social realities from what are often complex texts. The first step must be a close textual and literary analysis of the texts themselves, with the aim of understanding their individual rhetorical strategies.[73] There is a long way to go towards achieving this necessary end.

What then is the corpus of material to be studied?

Christian dialogues, to speak only of late antiquity, range from anti-Jewish texts (*Adversus Iudaeos*) to more apologetic works such as Minucius Felix's Latin *Octavius*,[74] or to the seeming scholasticism of Theodoret's *Eranistes* in the fifth century, for which see the discussion in chapter 3 below. The interlocutors may be pagans, or Jews, or Manichaeans, Zoroastrians, or, later, Muslims, and

---

[69] See Jacobs 2004.

[70] Jacobs 2007:295.

[71] Jacobs 2007:296-297. Hösle's distinction between the debate itself, and the written record, is philosophical rather than historical; he is concerned with the relation between art and meaning rather than what "actually happened."

[72] For a stronger view, see Siniossoglou 2008: chap. 1 on Theodoret's *Cure for Hellenic Maladies* and the nature of Christian apologetic.

[73] For the case of heresiology, see Averil Cameron 2003, 2005.

[74] On which, see Goldlust 2010:417-422.

the topics covered differ just as much. Yet I believe that these different types should be studied in conjunction with each other, not excluding more philosophical dialogues such as that between Zacharias Scholasticus and Ammonius on the eternity of the world, the dialogue on predestined terms of life by the early-eighth century patriarch Germanus[75] (preceded by another by the historian Theophylact Simocatta on the same topic nearly a century before),[76] or the highly rhetorical dialogue between history and philosophy which precedes the same Theophylact's history of the reign of the Emperor Maurice.[77] The anonymous Greek work *On Political Science* extant from the reign of Justinian is also a dialogue, based, even if indirectly, on Cicero's *De republica*, but also appealing to the memory of Socrates, and imbued with late antique Neoplatonism.[78] A self-conscious reference to the aims of "dialectical science" is put into the mouth of the character named Menas; they are, quite simply, to lead one to the divine.[79] There are also poetic dialogues from late antiquity, especially in Syriac, but also including the Greek sixth-century dialogue poems by Romanos.[80] These dialogues raise issues about liturgical performance, and questions of possible origin in Syriac rather than Greek contexts; there is also evidence for antiphonal singing in earlier Syriac religious literature.[81] The interesting types of dramatic dialogues represented in Romanos's liturgical hymns also found their way into Greek prose homiletics.[82]

While some of the literary prose dialogues owe a clear debt to Plato, others are very different. Joel Walker has drawn attention to the plethora of debates at the Sasanian court in the sixth century, and their debt to Aristotelian logic, to which I will return in the next chapter.[83] But again there is no simple historical progression, and the interplay between Platonic and Aristotelian elements is one of the still-untold stories in the long history of Greek Christian dialogue-writing from the second century to the end of the Byzantine era.

---

[75] Garton and Westerink 1979.

[76] Garton and Westerink 1978; discussion: Garton and Westerink 1979:xvi–xvii; Michael Whitby 1988:33–39; Michael Whitby and Mary Whitby 1986:xv (following the pattern of rhetorical *controversiae*); Frendo 1988:144–147.

[77] Michael Whitby 1988:40–45; Michael Whitby and Mary Whitby 1986:3–5; see Olajos 1981 for the argument that the dialogue did not originally belong with the *History* (I owe this reference to Elodie Turquois). Theophylact's *Problems of Natural History* (ed. Massa Positano 1965) is a further dialogue: Michael Whitby 1988:33–34; Michael Whitby and Mary Whitby 1986:xiv–xv.

[78] Bell 2009, 2013. Platonism in the dialogue: O'Meara 2002:49–62; O'Meara 2003.

[79] Bell 2009:181.

[80] Krueger 2003; Frank 2005; Brock 1984; 1987; 1991; Averil Cameron 1991a; Reinink 1991.

[81] See Harvey 2005.

[82] See Cunningham 2003:101–113.

[83] Walker 2006.

A final question concerns the types of writing in late antiquity that are not strictly dialogues in form, but which might be (and have been) held to embody the "dialogic," in that they express debates and arguments and differing points of view. Letters—very important in the corpus of Byzantine literature—certainly qualify, but I refer here rather to the sets of "questions and answers," or *erotapokriseis*, of which many survive with various degrees of literary finish or secure attribution. These vary between the scholastic and the more pastoral, and Andrew Jacobs has no hesitation in including one of the latter in his paper about dialogue—the *Questions to Antiochus the Dux* ascribed to Athanasius, a text which in its present form seems to date from the late seventh or eighth century.[84] Similar examples include works by Anastasius of Sinai in the seventh century, and the sixth-century collection attributed to Caesarius,[85] but the genre had begun much earlier, for instance with the fifth-century set of "Questions and answers to the orthodox," going under the name of Justin, and others are more didactic or even scholarly, like Eusebius's *Gospel Questions* (CPG 3470) and the later sets of *quaestiones* or *ambigua* by such writers as Maximus the Confessor.[86] The Christian examples form one part of a story that also encompasses both Jewish literature and philosophical texts.[87] Such sets of questions and answers between master and pupils, along with *zetemata* (inquiries on specific points) and *erotemata* (questions) were a regular part of the educational system at the grammarian's level.[88] All these types are receiving attention elsewhere, and my focus here is on the Platonizing or "philosophical" dialogues, while recognizing that the demarcation lines may well on occasion become blurred.

My contention, then, is that dialogue, as practiced by Christian writers, including Platonizing prose dialogues, did not end in the fifth century, or at any other time in the late antique and Byzantine periods, but was instead a vehicle for Christian expression that continued to be used for many centuries with enormous energy and variety. It contributed to the process of Christianization and the drive towards orthodoxy, and was a valuable tool for Christian writers. But the story is more complex than this suggests. Dialogue also interconnects with other kinds of Christian writing, and in turn, literary dialogues interconnect with "real" or actual debates, a subject that will be considered in my next chapter.

Entangled in this topic are several different strands. I have been concerned up to now with the purpose of Christian dialogues and their implications for the

---

84   See Jacobs 2007:328–332.
85   Riedinger 1989 (four sets of questions with designated speakers); Papadogiannakis 2008.
86   See below, chapter 3, on Theodoret.
87   See Volgers and Zamagni 2004; Bussières 2013; Papadoyannakis 2006, 2008; cf Niehoff 2008.
88   Cribiore 2001:207, 209–212.

development of thought and argument in the Christian empire. But they also raise philosophical and theological issues in varying degrees, and some at any rate can claim to be genuinely literary or rhetorical.[89] Should these therefore be seen as part of a so-called "Third Sophistic," the outpouring of high-style Greek literature in late antiquity, including many works by Christians, and if so, how far is a literary/rhetorical analysis appropriate?[90] It is at least worth asking the question, since Libanius, his circle, and the "Gaza school"[91] still receive disproportionate attention among literary theorists of late antiquity.

My third and final chapter will consider three very different examples in order to bring out the actual variety within this corpus, and the range of methodological approaches required to do it justice. It will also consider the increasing technologization perceptible in some later dialogues, and return to Richard Lim's question about what this may represent. Many questions remain, as well as a huge body of material from the later Byzantine period, much of which has hardly yet been studied, but which I hope to discuss in later publications. On the whole, Christian dialogues have been the subject only of individual studies or general surveys that are far from comprehensive.[92] I want to argue in contrast that this is a worthwhile, and indeed an important field, even if so far a neglected one, and that its study has great potential both for literary history and for our understanding of the religious and intellectual dynamics of late antiquity and beyond.

---

[89] Siniossoglou 2008:21–27, argues that the appropriation of ancient philosophy by Christian writers was "rhetorical" rather than doctrinal, that is, Christian apologists did not engage with the substance so much as the form. He also argues for a strongly essentialist understanding of both "Platonism" and "Christianity," on the basis of which he denies the possibility of "Christian Hellenism."

[90] See Averil Cameron, forthcoming a.

[91] See e.g. Saliou 2005; Amato 2010; for the production and educational environment at Gaza in the early sixth century, see Johnson, forthcoming.

[92] The most complete for late antiquity is Voss 1970. For the Byzantine period, see Ieraci Bio 2006.

2

Dialogue and Debate in Late Antiquity

I F, IN THE WORDS OF THE LATE KEITH HOPKINS, the Roman empire was a world full of gods,[1] late antiquity was a world full of talk. The known religious debates and discussions ranged from the discussions in major church councils and local synods, through public debates between Chalcedonians and Syrian Orthodox, against Manichaeans, pagans or heterodox Christians to the debating of individuals like Paul the Persian in the sixth century. Debate was the stuff of life. Witness John of Ephesus's account of the travelling Miaphysite holy man Symeon beth Arsham, who argued against heresy and debated with "Nestorians" in the lands beyond the Roman border in the east in the reign of Anastasius and later, and became known as "Simeon the Persian debater"; so great was his debating skill that early in his career Simeon allegedly won a contest with the east Syrian *catholicos* Babai.[2] We are here in a context in which Aristotelian logic was more to the point than Plato, as part of what has been called "an escalating philosophical 'arms-race.'"[3] This is an example of debate whose purpose was deadly serious, and whose techniques were greatly assisted by the scholastic formation now available in the east Syrian philosophical and theological schools. That relationship also worked in more than one direction: both east and west Syrians taught prospective debaters the tools of debate. The students of the School of Nisibis, for example, produced disputation texts against a variety of opponents—astrologers, Jews, magi, Miaphysites, and "heretics." Literally hundreds of students, to follow Joel Walker's account, learned Aristotelian logic in the School, and composed questions-and-answers as a preparation for writing disputations.[4] Barhadbešabba, a prominent member of

---

[1] Hopkins 1999; for similar comments, closer to our subject here, see Sizgorich 2009: chaps. 1 and 2, pointing out that written dialogues belong in a context of action.
[2] Brooks 1923–1925:1.138–139; see Becker 2006:47–48; Wood 2010:228–229; King 2012:69.
[3] Becker 2006:130; Lössl and Watt 2011.
[4] Walker 2006:187.

the School, wrote disputes and refutations of "all religions," the other side of which were the "defences" or apologies which he also composed.[5]

Daniel King has recently mounted the argument that the level of logical expertise was in fact low, and challenged the picture of scholastic activity painted by Jack Tannous for the monastic center at Qenneshre, on the west bank of the Euphrates, and elsewhere.[6] When employed, he maintains, the syllogistic reasoning was not at a genuinely philosophical level; moreover, he claims, many of these debates were politically sensitive and "usually a matter of making the right connections."[7] But the evidence for learned culture, of which the logical works of Aristotle were part, is too widespread to ignore or denigrate. Nor should the focus be directed only towards the east.

Richard Sorabji may claim of Zacharias Scholasticus's *Ammonius* that it reads "like a cabaret act designed to impress his fellow Christian students, with a catalogue of arguments that are mostly naïve and compressed";[8] yet such judgements suggest in fact that the question of Aristotelianism in relation to Christian authors needs more exploration than it has so far received. Sorabji takes the use of Christian *florilegia* as a sign of poor argumentation on Zacharias's part, and John Philoponus is indeed exempted from his criticisms. However no one would deny that sixth-century Alexandria maintained a high level of philosophical learning; moreover, as the Neoplatonist Simplicius's commentaries on the *Categories* and other works make clear, Aristotelian elements had also been admitted into late Neoplatonism,[9] while the extent to which Aristotle could be harmonized with Plato was already an issue in this period, just as it was in late Byzantium. It would be surprising if Christian authors were completely outside these trends.[10] Despite previous doubts about the patristic period and the "dark ages," it seems highly likely that basic Aristotelian logic continued to be taught in the Byzantine empire and in Constantinople, and it certainly formed an educational staple for the Byzantine period as whole. The philosophical quality of the argument in Christian dialogues from the late antique period to the end of Byzantium is a complex issue which in most specific cases still remains to be investigated; but it remains striking that the teaching of Aristotle's logical works becomes a more and more prominent feature.

---

[5] Walker 2006:91–92; cf. the "Disputation with Caesar" attributed to Paul of Nisibis (Walker 2006:92, and see below).

[6] King 2012; Tannous 2013; compare Lössl and Watt 2011.

[7] King 2012:70–78, cf. 70n44, citing Reinink 1999.

[8] Sorabji, preface, in Gertz et al. 2012:xxiii–xxiv.

[9] See also O'Meara 2002:206-7.

[10] Though brief, Saïd and Trédé 1999:171–179 contains useful suggestions for contextualizing common features in pagan philosophical and Christian works.

In relation to the real public debates that took place in the sixth and seventh centuries, King also maintains that "victory" had little to do with the quality of the argument, and that those sponsored by Justinian in Constantinople were "mostly for show."[11] We may of course allow for a high degree of manipulation or attempted manipulation of the events and the records (as in many instances in modern political life) but recent work on the preparation for and argumentation at the many synods and councils in this period suggests otherwise.[12] Such dismissive judgments simply fail to ask the basic question of why there were so many debates of so many different types and at so many different levels.

The literary sources also describe the debates in which famous schoolmen engaged on their travels, like that of Mar Aba in the sixth century with "Sergius" in Alexandria or with Zoroastrians in Seleucia/Ctesiphon, after which he is said to have founded the School of Seleucia.[13] While the latter story may well rank as a foundation myth, each kind of public debate had its counterpart in written debates and dialogues, which sometimes related to actual discussions (debates that "really took place"), but were also often composed independently. The relationship, if any, between these two types is not easy to establish, nor is it a simple matter.

Sixth-century Alexandria was also a center where, as we see from John Philoponus, Aristotelian syllogisms could be put to the service of Christian debate.[14] The twenty or more classrooms now exposed in the late antique complex in the Kom el-Dikka area in the city—perhaps the very site of Ammonius's teaching—show just how lively and active was the educational activity that went on there,[15] and some of this energy found expression in the production of Christian doctrinal and philosophical dialogues. One who composed dialogues on a variety of topics was Zacharias Scholasticus, author of a philosophical dialogue on the eternity of the world known as the *Ammonius*,[16] partly set in the lecture room of Ammonius himself during sessions about Aristotle's *Physics* and *Ethics*. The *Ammonius* contains three reported dialogues within a framing dialogue which is set in Beirut (Berytus), also a center of lively student life, as is famously described in Zacharias's *Life* of Severus of Antioch.[17] Zacharias also

---

[11] King 2012:68–69.
[12] For instance, see the two synods of 536 in Constantinople, discussed by Millar 2008 and 2009, and see below.
[13] See Becker 2006:157.
[14] See for instance Uthemann 1981a.
[15] Derda et al. 2007.
[16] Minniti Colonna 1973; Colonna 1958; Gertz et al. 2012; see Watts 2005a; 2005b; 2006:227–230; 2006–2007.
[17] Brock and Fitzgerald 2013.

wrote dialogues on Manichaeanism, and against the "sophists,"[18] and is one of the figures who can give us glimpses of the intense intellectual atmosphere of Alexandria, with its heady mix of pagan and Christian students, literary debates.

Manichaeanism provides a further background for this debating culture.[19] At the end of the fourth century, a story told in the *Historia monachorum in Aegypto* lets us see the extent to which the practice and utility of public debate was taken for granted: a certain Copres met at Hermopolis a Manichaean, "who had been leading the people astray." He engaged the Manichaean in a public trial by fire (in which Copres was successful), but only after he had "been unable to make him change his mind by debating with him in public."[20] A few years later Augustine debated against Felix the Manichaean in two sessions recorded by stenographers; this episode resulted in a formal abjuration (recantation) by Felix, in a formulaic statement of a kind that had a long life in subsequent centuries and into the Byzantine period.[21] This was not the first time that Augustine had taken on a Manichaean in public debate: in 392, both Catholics and Donatists in Hippo "urged" him to hold a public debate with the Manichaean Fortunatus, which took place over two days in the public baths and attracted a large crowd.[22]

Our surviving literature is full of set-pieces of debate (on that we can agree with King). Disputation features in the late fourth-century *Acta Archelai*.[23] According to this account, Mani debated with a bishop called Archelaus in Mesopotamia in the house of Marcellus, with four learned pagans as judges. Mani was defeated, and driven out of the town of "Carchar" by the crowd who had gathered to listen; here too the debate was recorded by stenographers and carefully written out.[24] At the end of the fourth century the controversial bishop Porphyry of Gaza is also said to have found himself debating with a Manichaean, this time a mature and confident woman called Julia, who came surrounded by four young and handsome supporters;[25] yet again, the proceedings were recorded by others. Ousted in the argument, Porphyry called on God to intervene, Julia was struck speechless and paralyzed, and quickly died. However sensational, this story tells us that such public argument was accepted and even expected in religious matters. It was assumed that the superiority of one faith

---

[18] PG 85.1011–1044.

[19] Lim 1995a:70–108; see also Stroumsa and Stroumsa 1988.

[20] *Historia monachorum in Aegypto* 10.30–35 (191–225), Festugière 1961:87–88; translation in S. N. C. Lieu 1992:185.

[21] Augustine *Against Felix*, cf. S. N. C. Lieu 1992:196–197.

[22] Augustine *Against Fortunatus*, CSEL XXV.I, 83–112; cf. also Baker-Brian 2009.

[23] S. N. C Lieu 1988:69–88.

[24] *Acta Archelai* 68.5, Beeson 1906:98.

[25] Grégoire and Kugener 1930:88; see Lim 1995a:84–87.

over another was demonstrable by reason, and the holding of such contests in public was an important part of religious rivalry in late antiquity.

Clearly the level and style of arguments like these would vary from setting to setting and from place to place. Augustine recognized the excitement and intellectual stimulus he had gained from such contests (*certamina*), just as he recognized the importance of having the right record-taker. Augustine's enjoyment of the challenge has been dismissed as attributable to youthful enthusiasm,[26] but his debates in Hippo against Fortunatus, Faustus and Felix required careful preparation and regard for his audience, which contained some who could well appreciate a reasonably sophisticated level of reasoning. In view of the tendency of Christians to resort to scriptural and patristic proof texts, it is interesting to find Augustine claiming that the audience in his debate with Fortunatus in AD 392 demanded rational argument, not lists of Scriptural precedents.[27] Again, the relationship between such actual debates and Christian polemical refutations of Manichaeism is complex,[28] involving questions both of the types of argument and the content, but it certainly existed. Both "real" and literary debates drew on the same background of expectation, even if not always to the same degree or in the same way. They have, admittedly, moved a long way away from the technique of Socratic questioning that Simon Goldhill takes as normative for dialogue.

Maijastina Kahlos connects this move, which we may characterize as taking us away from dialogue and towards dialectic, to the desire to set boundaries, part both of the effort of mission and conversion and the effort to achieve orthodoxy.[29] She asks whether actual dialogue was possible, when the object seems always to have been to win the argument;[30] sometimes, certainly, and for the sake of mission, a Christian would need to make an accommodation towards his opponents—to concede that they had some right on their side—or to descend to their level in order to move the argument forward, but the "exclusivist" model was the prevailing one.[31] Whether genuine "interreligious dialogue" took place, or was even possible, is a real question. Many of those who have studied the later Christian-Muslim debates have done so from the standpoint of modern ecumenism ("inter-faith dialogue"), and sometimes with a conscious desire to find some kind of harmonization.[32] The question of accom-

---

[26] Lim 1995a:90–91.

[27] Augustine *Against Fortunatus* 19, CSEL XXV, 97.

[28] For examples and discussion, see Stroumsa and Stroumsa 1988.

[29] Kahlos 2007:58–92; see also Sizgorich 2009:21–45.

[30] Kahlos 2007:75.

[31] Kahlos 2007:78–79.

[32] In the case of Christian-Jewish dialogues, the publisher of a recent work (Varner 2005) suggests that its "comprehensive spiritual index" will help to foster greater study of the place of these texts in the history of Jewish-Christian relations.

modation may apply more to the more philosophical dialogues and those than engage at a high literary level with pagan culture, and it is a question to which I will need to return; I would suggest, however, that it is best to leave doing so until after we have surveyed more of the very broad field of real and literary debates themselves.

Both Justinian and his contemporary and rival, the sixth-century Persian shah Chosroes I, were patrons of public debates. There were large numbers of Christians in Sasanian empire and in the sixth century they occupied important places at court and in high circles. Many pre-Islamic disputation texts by Christians are known, even if few have survived,[33] and the late sixth to early-seventh century Persian shah Chosroes II was a patron of the shrine of St. Sergius at Resafa and had a Christian wife. In an important recent study Joel Walker, following Antoine Guillaumont, has emphasized the fact that under Chosroes's father and predecessor Chosroes I many individuals from the Sasanian empire participated in religious debates held in Constantinople under the patronage of the Emperor Justinian.[34] One of them was a certain Paul the Persian, who debated with Photinus the Manichaean in Constantinople in 527.[35] The text of this debate survives (if it does indeed record what was said); it took place over several days, at the orders of the Emperors Justin and Justinian, and under the supervision of the illustrious *praeses* Theodorus. The cut and thrust of the debate itself is followed in the text printed in the Patrologia Graeca, which is all that is currently available, by formal statements from each side, reminiscent of the way in which Christian treatises against heresy, or synodical letters by bishops like the one issued by Sophronius as patriarch of Jerusalem in 634,[36] were followed by statements of orthodox doctrine. Justinian also invited east Syrians to debate in Constantinople, just as he had invited Syrian Miaphysites in the early years of his reign.[37] In the last years of Justinian, after the great peace treaty with the

---

[33] Excellent discussion in Walker 2006:169–180.

[34] See Guillaumont 1970 and 1969–1970.

[35] PG 88.529–552; a critical edition and English translation are in preparation: see Byard Bennett, "Paul the Persian," *Encyclopaedia Iranica*, s.v. (www.iranicaonline.org, accessed November 10, 2013). See also Morbe 2011. Bennett argues that Paul the Persian cannot be the same as the later author of an introduction to the logic of Aristotle composed for Chosroes I, and points out that there is no evidence that Theodorus was still prefect in 527. Junillus, author of a set of didactic questions and answers in Latin on Scriptural exegesis and Christian cosmology written under Justinian in the 540s, presents his work as inspired by the teachings and writings of Paul, a Persian from the School of Nisibis: see Maas 2003, who argues that Junillus was not merely reproducing Paul. Junillus explains his format in his prologue as representing the questions and answers between pupils and master, in which the master will be designated by the Greek letter M and the pupils by Δ (Maas 2003:120.13–18).

[36] Allen 2009.

[37] Brock 1981 (1992:XIII).

Sasanians in AD 562, a group from the Sasanian empire, who included the future catholicos Isho'yahb I and were led by a certain Paul of Nisibis, debated at the emperor's invitation in Constantinople; Paul left a record of their discussion (which does not survive but is discussed in a later text), known as the *Disputation with Caesar*.[38]

The Sasanian empire is also the context for the activities of "Symeon the Persian debater," whom we have already met, and the east Syrian theologian Babai the Great (d. c. 628) also records an intense level of debate between rival Christian groups continuing in the later sixth century.[39] As Walker describes, the Syriac church historian John of Ephesus, in his *Ecclesiastical History*, tells us that Chosroes I had instigated debates between Nestorians and Jacobites (that is, Miaphysites or Syrian Orthodox), whose numbers were increasing in the Persian empire. John claims that the king was himself convinced by the arguments of the Jacobite Ahudemmeh, and guaranteed the Jacobites protection. I quote the words John ascribes to him: "These men know what they say, and can establish and prove their words, and their arguments seem to me very true."[40] There are indeed some suspicious elements in the story, which suit John's own Miaphysite agenda, but the *mise-en-scène* and the debate itself ring true enough. And in AD 612, in the next reign, a series of debates between Nestorians and Jacobites was organized for Chosroes II by his Jacobite doctor.[41]

This context of genuine religious debate also lies behind the text of an imaginary "conference" set at the Persian court edited in 1899 by Eduard Bratke.[42] The subject is a debate between a pagan philosopher and two groups of Jews, Zoroastrians and a Christian bishop, over the status of Greek oracles. It was allegedly summoned by the Persian king, who appointed Aphroditian to settle the matter. This text may well be a "historicizing romance," as Cancik would have it, but we cannot doubt the existence of real debates in the Sasanian and east Mediterranean world, or the knowledge and practice of Aristotelian logic that was promoted in the schools.[43] Tannous is right to locate both major public debates and "small-time theological debates" in the context of intense religious rivalry and competition for adherents, which was accompanied by frequent "code-switching," changes or changing expressions of allegiance.[44] The circumstances of the sixth and seventh centuries, including the lengthy process

[38] Walker 2006:174n36; Maas 2003:18; Wood 2013a:53.
[39] Walker 2006:178.
[40] *Ecclesiastical History* 3, 6.20.
[41] Walker 2006:179.
[42] Bratke 1899; cf. Cancik 2008:7, and see Heyden 2009 and the doctoral thesis of P. Bringel, Paris, 2007.
[43] Walker 2006:187–188.
[44] Tannous 2013:93.

of the "separation" of the Syrian Orthodox,[45] thus played into an existing trend in Christian practice and Christian writing.

It was therefore entirely explicable, given this evidence for public theological debate, that the legendary text that is the subject of Walker's book should itself contain a scene of debate in which the hero engages in similar discussion. Its subject is one we have already encountered—the eternity of the heavenly bodies. This was a much-debated topic, whether by the so-called astrologers who are said to have debated with the late-sixth century stylite, Symeon the Younger,[46] or in the critique directed by John Philoponus in sixth-century Alexandria against Simplicius' argument for the eternity of the heavenly bodies, which had raised issues around the harmonization of Plato and Aristotle,[47] or the *Theophrastus* by Aeneas of Gaza and Zacharias Scholasticus's *Ammonius*. It also resonates with the dialogues we have already met which dealt with the question of whether God had foreordained how long each individual would live.

The seventh century was a key period for Christian debate. In the early 640s Maximus Confessor was living in a monastery at Carthage, North Africa, and on an earlier stay had responded in his correspondence to the distant news of the emergence of a new prophet in Arabia. Pyrrhus, the patriarch of Constantinople, was ousted from his seat in 641 after the death of the Emperor Heraclius in circumstances that are still imperfectly understood.[48] He left Constantinople for North Africa and in AD 645, very shortly before a coup was launched in the name of Gregory, the Byzantine exarch of Africa, Pyrrhus took part in a formal debate with Maximus in Gregory's presence in Carthage. The subject was the doctrine of Monothelitism, which Maximus opposed.[49] Maximus prevailed, and Pyrrhus departed for Rome to confess his recantation to the pope (though his "conversion" did not last very long and he briefly became patriarch again in 654). The Greek text survives at some length, and is clearly a justification of Maximus's position. Most students of Maximus have assumed that the debate actually

---

[45] Which tends to obscure the equally crucial role of the east Syrian Church of the East in the same period.

[46] Van den Ven 1962–1970:138–139.

[47] Discussion: Walker 2006:189–194, especially 191–194, with bibliography.

[48] Interventions from Rome combined here with imperial succession politics in Constantinople: see Booth 2013:262, 282–283. I am very grateful to Phil Booth for discussion and for generously allowing me to see his book in advance of publication.

[49] PG 91.288–353; Booth 2013:285–287; German translation and notes in Bausenhart 1992; unpublished text and French translation, Doucet 1972. Jankowiak 2013 argues that Dyothelitism, formulated in response to assertions of one will in Christ (Monothelitism), did not take shape until the early 640's, and that Monothelitism was not an "imperial doctrine" imposed by the *Ekthesis*; he also argues for 636 as the date of the *Ekthesis* against the usual 638. See Booth 2013 for a more gradualist view.

took place and that this is its record,[50] although according to J. Noret the text derives from the period of Maximus's exile in Thrace, in AD 655 or later, as part of Maximus's defense.[51] However we do not need to doubt the reality of the debate itself; Maximus is questioned about it in the *Record of the Trial*, one of the documents in the dossier relating to his exile and trial, and refers to recalling it from memory.[52] The debate consists in the main of Maximus's responses to questions and arguments offered by Pyrrhus, and includes detailed exegesis of citations from Cyril and others, including Ps. Dionysius.[53] The exarch Gregory, who very soon launched his own rebellion against Constantinople, arranged the debate, but did not intervene himself, except to agree with Maximus in conclusion about the need for Pyrrhus to profess his orthodoxy before the pope.[54] As it stands, the debate is an important theological document, part of a highly complex developing situation. It is remarkable, in the words of Phil Booth, that "despite holding no clerical position, Maximus debates the faith in open, reasoned dialogue with a (deposed) patriarch."[55]

The affair was also highly political: it was assumed by Maximus and Gregory that Pyrrhus's recantation required the ratification of Rome, and he and Maximus went there together.[56] Maximus's position challenged the status and ecclesiastical policies of Constantinople as surely as Gregory's "rebellion." If the text of the debate was indeed a later production, it nevertheless envisaged a situation in which it was possible to contemplate just such a public debate in Greek being held in mid-seventh century Carthage in the tense and highly charged atmosphere before Gregory's revolt and immediately before Maximus's departure for Rome and the Lateran Synod of 649. It is impossible now to know whether the debate really happened as reported; but perhaps after all this is not the point.

---

[50] That such a public debate should have taken place in Greek in Carthage is striking, though Greek had indeed come into use alongside Latin in the course of the Byzantine reconquest in 534; eastern saints were venerated and refugees from the Persian invasion of the eastern Mediterranean in the early seventh century had led to an increase in the presence of Greek-speakers like Maximus in monastic communities in North Africa. For Maximus's own associates, see Booth 2013:153–154.

[51] Discussion in Allen and Neil 2002:15–18, Jankowiak 2013:342, Noret 1999; see Van Deun 2009:101–104.

[52] Allen and Neil 2002:61; for critical editions of the *Record* and the debate with Theodosius, see Allen and Neil 1999.

[53] For the use of patristic authorities in the debate over Monothelitism, see Bausenhart 1992:182–192, with 192–193 on the debate with Pyrrhus; several *florilegia* are attributed to Maximus.

[54] PG 91.353A.

[55] Booth 2013:286.

[56] PG 91.352D–353B.

There is another seeming dialogue among the documents relating to the trials and exile of Maximus, presented as the record of a lengthy debate held in formal circumstances at Bizya during his exile in Thrace in AD 656 between Maximus and Theodosius, a local bishop.[57] After the first episode both speakers pray and kiss the Gospel, the cross and the icon of the Virgin and Child in order to seal their discussion.[58] The text defends Maximus by emphasizing his willingness to be reconciled with the imperial authorities, and we are told that the consul Theodosius goes away imagining that this is possible.[59] But Maximus is then moved to another monastery, and two patricians with imperial orders arrive and reopen the discussion. Although the dilemma of the bishop Theodosius, Maximus' earlier interlocutor, is depicted with some nuance, this time Maximus provokes the officials to anger and physical abuse, and he is moved again, first to an army camp at Selymbria and then to be tried in Constantinople and eventually mutilated. What we have here is a complex series of debates embedded in an apologetic account of the sufferings of Maximus and his disciples.[60] Like the earlier debate with Pyrrhus, that between Maximus and Theodosius also deploys patristic citations in its argumentation, a feature central to Christian debate since the fifth century.

How far we should consider this to be a dialogue is questionable, although "disputation" (from its Latin title) does not seem to fit it very well either. It is more like a forensic questioning, and is embedded within the pro-Maximus dossier since it took place in the context of an official delegation sent to him in his place of exile. We also meet here an imperial reaction to a level of debate that was clearly considered out of control—an order to stop any discussion. Such an order was included in the *Typos* (decree) issued by the patriarch Paul in AD 647 or 648; it followed earlier precedents and it was equally unsuccessful.[61] But in such an atmosphere of disagreement and emotion, debate and religious argument were simply impossible to control. In any case such orders were designed for symbolic rather than actual effect.

By the seventh century the practice and habit of debate, or dialogue, was thoroughly embedded in religious interchanges. But it received another enormous extra impetus as a result of the Monenergist (one energy) and Monothelite (one will) doctrines pushed by Constantinople under the Emperor Heraclius and his grandson and successor Constans II.[62] The collection of sources for the

---

[57] Allen and Neil 2002:77–119. A variety of terms are in use in the manuscript tradition of dialogues, including *dialogos* and *dialexis*, and in Latin, *disputatio*.
[58] Allen and Neil 2002:100.
[59] Allen and Neil 2002:104.
[60] The trial of 662: Allen and Neil 2002:25.
[61] Earlier attempts to shut down argument: Lim 1995a:219, 227.
[62] So Cubitt 2009:133–147; see now Booth 2013.

controversy compiled in 1987 by Friedhelm Winkelmann indicates the level of debate, which in its earlier stages had also involved Sophronius, the eventual patriarch of Jerusalem.[63] Debates, dialogues and disputations appear under varying descriptions and titles, and the sheer overall quantity of argument and discussion is striking—no wonder the emperors tried to silence it. Though it is impossible to cover them here for reasons of space, I believe that we must also read the dialogues between Christians and Jews from this period and others, which are usually treated in isolation, against this context, as well as the incipient genre of debates between Christians and Muslims. A benefit of the broader approach advocated here is that it would challenge the over-simplified view that draws a line of intellectual transmission from Alexandria through Syria to Baghdad, while ignoring Constantinople.[64]

Dialogue and debate were features of the whole eastern Christian world, and the wealth of such material in Syriac should, certainly in the seventh century, be read in the whole east Mediterranean context. With the move to Sicily and Italy of Greek-speaking monks and clergy under pressure of the invasions of Palestine in the early seventh century, and the arrival in Rome of Maximus and his companions after his debate with Pyrrhus in Carthage, the Greek debating culture also reached Rome,[65] where a series of Greek popes carried on opposition to Monothelitism, and later to Byzantine iconoclasm. We are here genuinely in a world of disputation and debate.

Maximus's debate at Bizya in Thrace has a further dimension. In the dossier it precedes an account of his trial and punishment and is reminiscent, if in a more concrete form, of the debates in martyr accounts and hagiography. At the same time this blurring of boundaries brings us into the sphere of legal process and proof. During the period from the fifth century onwards we see a steadily increasing reliance in theological debates on proof texts, *florilegia* from the Fathers or from Scripture, specially compiled, and indeed eventually often manipulated or even faked.[66] Theological treatises, of which there are countless numbers, very often came with their own *florilegium* appended; other *florilegia* circulated separately, and were used, added to and adapted by others;[67] the same phenomenon is found in Syriac, drawing on translated Greek citations.[68]

---

[63] Winkelmann 1987, 2001 and see Allen 2009. Sophronius is defended by Maximus in the debate with Pyrrhus: PG 91.333B–C, with Bausenhart 1992:273–274, 276.

[64] See Lössl and Watt 2011.

[65] Booth 2013:290n51. Rome and the Lateran Synod of 649: Cubitt 2009; Greek émigrés in Italy and Sicily: Sansterre 1983; see Johnson, forthcoming for the inclusion of 'Nestorians' in this move to Rome from North Africa.

[66] The fundamental study is Richard 1951 (2011); see below, chapter 3 on Theodoret *Eranistes*.

[67] See Richard 1951 (2011), and cf. Alexakis 1996.

[68] See Rucker 1933: introduction. I will return to the subject of *florilegia* in chapter 3.

In general, the resort to proof texts, the choice of the proof texts to be used, and the crystallization of accepted lists of approved patristic writers to support this or that side in the argument, are striking developments of this period. This was all the more necessary as the stakes were set higher and higher for individuals in the period after the Council of Chalcedon in 451, involving for bishops a real possibility of deposition, exile, and anathemas, and indeed leading to the separation of the Miaphysites during the sixth century and later. As we saw, Tannous has drawn attention to the competitive religious environment in the Syrian context, and an equivalent situation is readily apparent from the seventh and eighth-century Greek question-and-answer literature by Anastasius of Sinai and others.

A key development in the scholarship of the last few years has been an upsurge of interest in the church councils of this period, and their argumentation and their proceedings. This has been greatly assisted by the publication in 2005 of a complete English translation of all the materials pertaining to the Council of Chalcedon, and another in 2009 on the council of AD 553 in Constantinople.[69] Also important are the critical editions of the Lateran Council of AD 649 and the Sixth Council of AD 680–681 by Rudolf Riedinger in the Acta Conciliorum Oecumenicorum; together they mark a very distinct step forward in awareness of the technicalities and complexities of all this material, as well as its potential for the historian.[70] In the sixth century, the Council of Constantinople, held in 553, was conspicuous for its reliance on such proof-texts and on the enormous effort that went into prior systematic preparation, and the example was followed in the succeeding ones.[71] The questions to ask about our dialogues and debates, therefore, concern the nature of their relation not merely to social reality, but also very importantly, to the formal proceedings of councils and synods and the argumentation and techniques used there. Not only was a considerable production of technical record-keeping required, as well as translation and the dissemination of copies, but also a high degree of technical knowledge and scholastic and legal argument.[72] The many dialogues and debates of the sixth and seventh centuries need to be placed against the background of a whole industry of technical argument and recording which these councils required and encouraged.

---

[69] Price and Gaddis 2005; Price, 2009.

[70] For the Acts of the Second Council of Nicaea (787), see Lamberz 2008. Annotated translations of the Lateran Synod (649), the Sixth Council (680–681) and II Nicaea (787) are in train in the TTH series.

[71] Cubitt 2009 discusses their technical management, in particular in relation to the controversial Lateran Synod of 649.

[72] See Humfress 2007 and Engels and Van Nuffelen 2014.

Christian dialogues embrace an enormously wide range of types, from the literary and philosophical to the technical, and their purposes and immediate aims, like the reasons for their composition, are equally wide-ranging. In the case of the question and answer literature and related texts, scholars have emphasized the motive of instruction, including catechesis.[73] Christian dialogues have also been seen as apologetic or polemical vehicles for sectarian agendas, or simply as "instrumental" texts.[74] These characterizations have truth in them, though they fail to acknowledge the actual variety of what we are dealing with. We can however accept that as the Christian dialogue form developed it became more and more closely embedded in the effort that went into the attempt to establish a single orthodoxy. Christian dialogues did have an object, and that object was to assert the author's conception of orthodox belief. Exegesis and selective citation were paramount. Inevitably such dialogues also tended to adopt the techniques of polemic or apologetic, and thus they became part of a vast and tangled array of textual practices designed to combat heresy and assert Christian truth. They were, I would argue, part of a much wider systematization of Christian knowledge. The rhetoric that many of them used was designed to abuse, attack and pour scorn on their targets.[75] In this sense such dialogues were as important as theological treatises or council decisions in the formation of opinion on doctrinal matters.

The question must be asked, therefore, how much such writings contributed to a growth of religious intolerance—leading at times to actual religious violence—in late antiquity. Reacting against such assumptions, several scholars recently have been seeking examples of religious tolerance in late antiquity, or if not that, then what at least we might call religious neutrality.[76] Richard Lim, again, has asked the reasonable question whether the often harsh debates between Christians in late antiquity contributed to the actual religious violence which is also a feature of the period; he points to several contemporary expressions of disapproval of dialectic which seem to indicate a similar anxiety.[77] Indeed, faced with the shrill rhetoric of late antique Christian texts, in which I include those written in dialogue form, it is hard not to conclude that even if they were not always successful in achieving their ostensible aims their objective was indeed usually aggressive. I have had occasion to part company with

---

[73] Cf. Munitiz 1988.

[74] Lim 1991; Garzya 1981.

[75] For late antique invective, see Kahlos 2009; Flower 2013.

[76] See Kahlos 2009; tolerance on the part of Constantine, intolerance on that of his bishops: Drake 2000; see also Averil Cameron 2002a; Ando 1996; Athanassiadi 2010 and some of the essays in Gwynn and Bangert 2010. A recent research project led by Kate Cooper asks whether monotheism must inevitably lead to violence.

[77] Lim 1995b.

Lim earlier, but his work is important because it takes religious debate seriously and on its own terms, without reducing it to a mere social or cultural manifestation. I agree entirely with him when he says that Christian debates introduced a new level of "verbal cognitive disagreement," or dissonance, into late antique cities (and not only cities).[78] I disagree with him in that whereas he would put a chronological terminus on it, in my view this cognitive disagreement intensified in the very period when Lim suggests that it was silenced;[79] it continued, moreover, not only through the turmoil of the seventh century and the rise of the new religion of Islam, but for many centuries to come.

In her study already cited, Maijastina Kahlos has focused on issues of Christian rhetoric and Christian intolerance in relation to late fourth- and early fifth-century writing, not considering dialogue forms as such but rather, Christian writing and debate in general.[80] Her main concern is also with Christian-pagan debate rather than doctrinal dialogue or Christian-Jewish texts. But she addresses in particular the rhetorical strategies used by Christian authors, and asks the question, "is genuine dialogue possible?" I quote: "Because mission was an essential part of ancient Christianity, Christians had to aim at a dialogue with non-Christians. A mere debate was not enough."[81] She is careful to define her terms, and as I said, she is not writing about the dialogue as a literary form; for her, "true" dialogue, though, as defined by sociologists of religion, or by practitioners of "dialogue analysis," and by contemporary advocates of pluralistic theology, exists when the two sides exchange views and arrive at a mutually agreed conclusion, incorporating modifications on both sides. This is, of course, the aim of modern consensual dialogue. It has indeed been argued that there can be such a thing as genuinely pluralistic theology, an idea to which responses have been sharp and negative.[82] On this basis, however, the "missionary dialogue" of ancient Christian writers is not dialogue, but pedagogy.

Some at any rate of the dialogues I am considering thus come nearer to monologue, and a patronizing or hostile monologue at that, and justify Kahlos's subtitle, "Dialogue and otherness"; they act to set and confirm boundaries, to impose distinctions.[83] In her two recent books[84] Kahlos deals with a stage (late fourth to early fifth centuries) when it was still an urgent necessity for Christians to engage with pagans; the apologetic need had not yet subsided. She has also

---

[78] Lim 1995b:229.

[79] For the debates and rivalries of this period, see Blaudeau 2006.

[80] Kahlos 2007.

[81] Kahlos 2007:75.

[82] See Hick and Knitter 1987, with D'Costa 1990, which contains critical papers by more conservative authors including A. McGrath and J. Milbank.

[83] On which, see Kahlos 2007:58–75.

[84] See also Kahlos 2012.

analyzed some of the typical rhetorical ploys used even in more "moderate" Christian writings in order to denigrate their opponents, an approach on which much more can be done. It would be a mistake however to assume a steady chronological development towards a more stereotyped and harsher tone as the subject matter moved towards doctrinal issues.

Two rather different issues have emerged in this chapter. First, I have tried to bring out both the intense level of actual debate during late antiquity, including many examples of public formal debate, and the very wide range of types and subjects it covered, from philosophical to religious. Second, as well as considering the issue of intolerance, I have continued to emphasize the huge number of surviving dialogue texts, some much more literary than others, many of them yet to be critically edited and studied. My third chapter, entitled "Writing Dialogue," will draw on some specific examples in order to bring out the variety of literary types existing in this corpus. How do the literary dialogues relate to "real" debates? This is a natural question, and one that has been asked many times in relation to the Christian-Jewish dialogues, not least by scholars who are interested in the actual relations between Christians and Jews in late antiquity. I am tempted to say that the question is misguided: we rarely have evidence outside the dialogue in question that would allow us to know the answer, and arguments drawn from the supposed plausibility of an internal scenario are dangerous indeed.

We have also seen an increasing technologization of dialogues, and some would say, a marked level of intolerance at least in certain examples, represented in the selective use of supporting materials and indicative of the high stakes affecting both intellectual and religious competition. Whether or not there was a connection between this expressed intolerance and the religious violence common in late antique cities is a much deeper question, as is the extent to which late antique culture was itself agonistic.

These remarks suggest by way of conclusion a brief further consideration of the principles behind my contention that it is important to study the Christian texts composed in dialogue form. I approach them neither as a theologian nor as a conventional patristic scholar, but as a historian who, I hope, is also sensitive to literary issues. As a historian, I am not seeking useful historical information from them, nor am I trying to write a social history. Nor, though I have been termed a "cultural historian," do I think I am simply doing cultural history, if that means considering Christian texts without their theological component.[85] These compositions are as much part of late antique and Byzantine literature as any secular texts, and they deserve a literary approach. But they also belong to

---

[85] Cf. E. A. Clark 2008a, especially 25–26.

the field of the history of religion. In terms of the formalization of a Christian knowledge system, and in order to understand the development of Christianity and the process of Christianization in late antiquity, as well as the workings of "Orthodoxy" in the later centuries of Byzantium, the study of these dialogues belongs within the striking move in the study of late antiquity in recent decades towards awareness of Christian texts as shaping historical development.

My focus here is on texts and their context, but in broader terms, dialogue, argument and debate were indispensable in the early Christian world. The need was philosophical, cultural and theological, and it intensified as time went on: debates produced other debates. This chapter has explored certain kinds of dialogue texts and the historical context from which they came, as well as some of the factors that led to their production. The context for others in the long history of Christian dialogues was quite different, as were the dialogues themselves. But the "literary" or "linguistic" turn can no longer be ignored in late antique studies. How Christians wrote, why they wrote as they did, and why they continued to do so over so many centuries and with such passion are crucial questions for historians, literary scholars and students of religion alike.[86]

---

[86] See especially E. A. Clark 2004, with review-discussion by Burrus et al. 2005.

3

Writing Dialogue

IN MY FINAL CHAPTER I will discuss three very different examples of Greek Christian dialogue-writing, two of them from the late antique period, the third composed later, but with a dramatic date in late antiquity. The first has attracted attention already, but is so unusual that it deserves its place here. The second also seems unusual, but was followed by other examples of not dissimilar type; it also illustrates an important feature of Christian argumentation. The third case I will consider may be included among the anti-Jewish dialogues, though it is a far from typical one. All three may be regarded as exceptional, yet at the same time highly suggestive. These cases cover only some of the many questions and lines of inquiry arising from our subject, but they point to the sheer variety as well as to some of the possibilities and directions inherent in this very wide-ranging way of writing.

The first author to be considered is Methodius, apparently from Olympus in Lycia and living in the late third and early fourth centuries. Much has been written about Methodius already, although little is known about his life, not even whether he was actually a bishop, as Jerome says.[1] He is best known as the author of the *Symposium*, but three other dialogues are attributed to him, not so well preserved, on free will, on the resurrection and on creation. All Methodius's dialogues are literary and ostensibly Platonizing; however, one of his main aims was to engage with the ideas of Origen (also the author, or perhaps rather the subject of reports of actual discussions, of a dialogue dealing with the Father and the Son, bodily resurrection and the soul).[2]

By far the best known of Methodius's dialogues is the *Symposium*, and while it is known particularly for reasons other than its dialogue form, its status as a

[1]   See Musurillo and Debidour 1963:9–11. I am indebted in the discussions of Methodius and Theodoret that follow to the excellent work done by my research assistant Alberto Rigolio; I am also grateful to Virginia Burrus for letting me see her paper on the *Symposium* in advance of publication, to Dawn La Valle for stimulating discussion and to Ryan C. Fowler for helpful email communication. For some of the material in this chapter, see also Averil Cameron, forthcoming a.

[2]   For which see Eusebius *Ecclesiastical History* 6.33, 37. Origen's dialogue with Heraclides: Scherer 1960, English translation, Daly 1992:57–78.

dialogue has currently come to the fore. The *Symposium* covers a wide range of topics, including Scriptural exegesis and eschatology, but the dialogue as a whole offers an extended argument for virginity as a means to attaining Christian virtue and the ascent of the soul. It has therefore attracted a large literature from scholars interested in questions of asceticism, gender, and virginity in early Christianity, and Elizabeth Clark has treated it more than once as a key text in the development of Christian literary, and especially gender, discourse.[3] Even though Scriptural allusions far outweigh classical ones in the text, it is obvious that it is modeled in some sense on Plato's *Symposium*, which had a long afterlife as a prototype for certain kinds of literary dialogue.

The *Symposium* is one of the few Christian dialogues which feature in more general discussions, for example in the book by Vittorio Hösle already mentioned, where Methodius's *Symposium* is cited as part of the story of the reception of Plato's dialogue of the same name.[4] Methodius does indeed reveal himself as a writer of literary ambition. In the *Symposium* he substitutes chastity for Plato's *eros* as the theme,[5] and goes much further than Gregory of Nyssa's *De anima* in making not just the central character but all the speakers female. The dialogue is set in a garden belonging to a lady called Virtue (*Arete*),[6] the daughter of Philosophy, who is very beautiful and is dressed in white, "like a mother greeting us after a long absence," while the participants in the discussion are ten virgins. The setting and *dramatis personae* recall not only the *Symposium* and *Phaedrus* but also the wise virgins in Matthew 25:10,[7] and the dialogue ends with an iambic hymn with an acrostic, addressed to Christ the Bridegroom. The naming of the leading virgin as Thecla is both literary and deliberate, with a clear reminiscence of the apocryphal Acts of Paul and Thecla, where Thecla stands for the power of virginity—she is described as having been instructed in "divine and evangelical doctrine" by St. Paul himself. In one of the common features of literary dialogue, the main conversation is reported—two women, Euboulion and Gregorion,[8] meet and in response to the other's invitation Gregorion recounts[9] what she had been told by Theopatra, one of

---

3   E. A. Clark 1999; 1995:364, "a treatise probably composed in the early years of the fourth century"; 2008b; 2009; Goldhill 1995:1-4, 43-44.

4   For instance Hösle 2012:450-451 and often.

5   Musurillo and Debidour 1963:50n2; Zorzi 2002, 2003, both accessed 22.1.13; Nygren 1953.

6   It is intriguing that the addressee of one of Iamblichus's letters, on self-control (*sophrosune*), is also called Arete: see Dillon and Polleichtner 2010, *Letter* 3. For the setting of the *Symposium* as a *locus amoenus*: Hösle 2012:231; for König 2012:156, 159, it is a "fantasy space," and the protagonists constitute a "fantasy community."

7   Prologue, 7-8. English translation, Musurillo 1958.

8   Methodius also uses the name Euboulios elsewhere, seemingly in reference to himself.

9   For the trope of a dialogue within a dialogue see Goldlust 2010:98; dramatic (direct) and reported (indirect, narrative) dialogues: Hösle 2012:166-168.

those present and the speaker of the fourth discourse,[10] about a banquet held at Arete's house, when Arete had invited each of the ten guests to compete for a prize by delivering a speech in praise of virginity (*parthenia*); each speech is presented as a *logos*, without dialogic introduction. One of the speakers argues that marriage is not inferior to virginity while another adopts the Pauline teaching whereby marriage is the lesser state, allowed because of human weakness. Their themes range from Old and New Testament exegesis to philosophy, allegory and eschatology.[11]

Not surprisingly, in view of her name and associations, Thecla is declared the winner, having spoken in eschatological terms about the Church.[12] She and Arete then take the lead in the stanzas of a remarkable acrostic hymn in iambics while the remaining ladies sing the refrain. In the hymn Thecla addresses Christ, who is addressed in the refrain as the Bridegroom, and cites in successive stanzas an interesting list of Scriptural *exempla* of virtue, and especially of chastity: Abel, Joseph, the daughter of Jephtha, Judith, Susanna, John the Baptist, and the Virgin Mary. Representing the choir of bridesmaids, Thecla addresses Christ as "the young bridegroom," and the "virginal" Church. Chastity is enthroned in heaven and Thecla alludes to her own martyrdom. The reported dialogue having concluded, with three short interludes between Euboulion and Gregorion and a few touches aiming at verisimilitude,[13] the two original speakers draw the work to a close in a framing epilogue (itself a dialogue on the soul that balances the introduction), referring to a mysterious lady from Telmessos in Lycia, who apparently provided Methodius's inspiration.

As the text's editor points out, the speeches in the *Symposium* are far more homiletic and didactic than dialectical, although there is a small attempt at genuine exchange between Marcella and Theophila.[14] The textual strategies that Methodius employs to advocate virginity include an adventurous attitude to passages in the Old Testament, a strongly Pauline emphasis, for instance in the use of I Corinthians 7:37 in the speech of Thalia,[15] and praise of virgins as the "brightest lights" mentioned in I Corinthians 15:41 and the "dove" in Song of

---

[10] Where she explicitly cites Psalms 136 and other Old Testament passages and expounds the meaning of the rivers of Babylon; as Musurillo points out, Arete's garden is a replica of Paradise and the banquet is an eschatological banquet (Musurillo and Debidour 1963:15).

[11] See Musurillo and Debidour 1963:14–19, and on Methodius and Plato, pp. 23–25.

[12] *Symposium*, discourse 8, para. 181, Musurillo and Debidour 1963:210.

[13] For instance in the first interlude Euboulion exclaims at the length of Thalia's speech ("an ocean of words"), and Gregorion encourages her to persist and listen to the others; Theopatra has told her that she herself spoke next, and her speech follows. In the third intervention, between the ninth and tenth speeches, both speakers fear for the understandable nervousness of Domnina, who is yet to speak and has to compete with all the others who have already spoken.

[14] Musurillo and Debidour 1963: paras. 34–40, pp. 75–79.

[15] Musurillo and Debidour 1963: discourse 3, paras. 91–92, pp. 125–126.

Songs 6.8–9 (the latter a passage used by Epiphanius, also a reader of Methodius, in his *Panarion*).[16]

The *Symposium* is a strange text. Vittorio Hösle finds in Methodius some fertile material for comparison, but he does not attempt to square the circle by putting the dialogue in its historical or theological context. Methodius also has unusually high literary ambitions. The *Symposium* does not fit the usual pattern of controversialist Christian dialogues, and has been read as a sympotic dialogue, with a large number of speakers each making an intervention.[17] Jason König even regards it as "our best surviving example of Christian sympotic writing." König is willing to allow to Methodius a rather subtle engagement with the agonistic features of sympotic dialogue and compares Methodius and Macrobius in their shared "cautious" transformative attitude to traditions of sympotic polyphony.[18] Within this sympotic frame, Methodius has boldly transferred the male world of Platonic dialogue (Diotima excluded) to a female one, while at the same time transforming Plato's homoerotic undertones and his discussion of *eros* into a paean to Christian chastity.

On the other hand, despite König's comparison of Methodius with Athenaeus and Macrobius, I would argue that the *Symposium* has little in common with the world of high-level literary conversation that we find for example in Athenaeus's *Deipnosophists*, expounded so elegantly in this series for both Athenaeus and Plutarch by Christian Jacob.[19] Richard Lim is also less than convincing when he suggests that the *Symposium's* sympotic dress links it to the cultic context of common meals among early Christians, "a shared sympotic or convivial context among his Christian readers that was very different from that of the usual readers of literary and philosophical dialogues."[20] König himself struggles with his sympotic reading. As he admits, there is not much food in Methodius's *Symposium*, unless allegorical. Methodius "distorts and defamiliarises ... in order to produce a distinctively Christian mode," and we read that his engagement with the techniques of sympotic conversation and debate is "rather anxious" and "ambivalent."[21] It is not surprising, then, that there is nothing else quite like it; on this basis, Methodius's experiment was a failure.

---

[16] E. A. Clark 1999:147–148, 286, 288, 352.

[17] See König 2009:98, 104; cf. 102–113; König 2012:151–176; Bril 2005; Hoffmann 1996:121–130.

[18] König 2009:106, 112, cf. 113: both authors are "engaging with those [sympotic] traditions intricately, reshaping them for their own new contexts and new uses." For Macrobius see König 2012:chap. 8 and Goldlust 2010.

[19] Jacob 2012. There were many different ways of referencing Plato's *Symposium*, as Jacob's discussion of Athenaeus makes clear (Jacob 2012:27), and Methodius's was all his own.

[20] Lim 2009:159.

[21] König 2012:165; cf. also 171–172 on the uncertainty between competitiveness and consensus in the dialogue, and 175, where König admits that Methodius's engagement with

We need to read the *Symposium* in the context of Methodius's other known dialogues. These are variously preserved: the dialogue *On Free Will* (*De autexousio*), probably earlier than the *Symposium*, survives in an Old Slavonic translation but only partially in Greek; *On the Resurrection* (*Aglaophon*), in three books, also survives in Slavonic translation, near-complete, with the Greek and Syriac in fragments; it alludes to Plato's *Protagoras* as well as to the *Phaedo* and *Symposium*, and, like the dialogue on free will and the *Symposium*, also to Homer; finally the *Xeno*, criticizing Origen's view of eternal creation, and known only from Photius.[22] Given the state of their transmission, it is hard to judge the literary quality of the three dialogues apart from the *Symposium*, but they too are ambitious. *Aglaophon*, or *On the Resurrection*, for instance, is long, and the dialogue is reported in the first person by Euboulius, representing the point of view of Methodius. Its opening is also Platonizing. The dialogue is staged in Patara in Lycia, in the house of the physician Aglaophon, who had converted the vestibule of the house into a hospital. Here Theophilus was "philosophizing" on the nature and resurrection of the body while sitting in an armchair (219.9, 13), by "answering the questions" (219.13–220.1) of Sistelius, Auxentius, Memmianus, Aglaophon and other "citizens" who sat on the floor; in just such a scene in Plato's *Republic*, the aged Cephalus, the father of Polemarchus, sits in a cushioned chair with others ranged around him in a semicircle in his son's house in the Peiraeus. Methodius's dialogue begins with the arrival of Eubulius, accompanied by Proclus from Miletus, who, on the same pattern as in Methodius's dialogue on free will, is presented as a companion of the main speaker with opposing views. Soon Eubulius is chosen as the judge of the contest (220.5–6). *Aglaophon* contains allusions to the *Phaedo*, *Protagoras*, *Symposium*, and *Phaedrus*. Both this and *On Free Will* (in which an orthodox speaker debates with two heterodox) refer self-consciously to their dialogic presentation, and in *On Free Will* the orthodox speaker puts the questions.

Methodius's works found readers, including the author of the anonymous dialogue known as *Adamantius* (ca. 330?) dealing with Marcionites, Bardesanites and Valentinians.[23] Methodius's work was used by Epiphanius of Salamis, author of the *Panarion* (370s), and his dialogues feature in later *florilegia*, in Syriac and Slavonic translations and in Photius.[24] Methodius's eschatology found a resonance

---

"traditional Greco-Roman ideas of sympotic playfulness and sympotic contest" was "not entirely comfortable."

[22] Surviving and reconstructed text: Bonwetsch 1891, with Buchheit 1958 and Patterson 1997. In general on Methodius, see Bracht 1999; 2011

[23] See E. A. Clark 1992:168–170; English translaton by Pretty, in Trompf 1997.

[24] *On the Resurrection* found its way into the Syriac *Florilegium Edessenum* (Rucker 1933:10–12). But the Slavonic translations seem to derive from confusion of this Methodius with the later "apostle to the Slavs."

in the late seventh-century Syriac *Apocalypse* of Ps. Methodius, wrongly ascribed to our Methodius. Finally, it has been argued that literary elements in *On Free Will* were imitated by the early seventh-century poet George of Pisidia.[25]

Methodius thus emerges both as an advocate of asceticism and a critical reader of Origen;[26] to use Goldhill's words, he has taken Plato's *eros* and set it within "the Christian parameters inscribed paradigmatically" in the *Symposium*, laying his emphasis on the virtue of *sophrosune*.[27] But Methodius was also a dialogue-writer of literary pretensions who, it seems, made a deliberate choice to cast his work in this form, perhaps influenced by Origen's own dialogue, and clearly with literary as well as philosophical and theological aims. What is interesting is that the same Methodius also wrote works that were *not* in dialogue form—something that is also characteristic of other dialogue-writers, including my next example. We tend to forget how enormous and varied was the output of Christian writers in the late antique period.[28] The totality of Christian writing is colossal, and within it dialogues are only a small part (debate and argument in the broader sense occupy much more space). We need not only to analyse the surviving dialogues for their own sake but also to place them within the context of the much wider body of Christian writing, as well as in the work of the individual author.

The puzzle of Methodius is that he remains so obscure as a historical personage, albeit one who has achieved a certain fame among modern scholars, if mainly for the very oddity of his *Symposium*. He may have misunderstood Origen, and his philosophy is hardly at the level of Plato, but a seventh-century epigram praises him for "opening the mouth of *logismoi* and bringing in the grace of the Holy Spirit."[29] He was read and translated by Rufinus into Latin in the cause of anti-Origenism, and into Slavonic. He was an energetic if somewhat mysterious writer and exegete, and there was more to him than gender and asceticism. Even though he is not one of the rhetoricians included by some scholars in a Third Sophistic,[30] he deserves at least a marginal place in the history of late antique and Christian literature.

My second Greek example is deliberately chosen as a contrast. It is also later in date (mid-fifth century), much more directly controversialist, and far less literary. This is Theodoret's *Eranistes*, usually dated to ca. 447. Theodoret himself was soon afterwards forbidden by the Emperor Theodosius II to leave

---

[25] Franchi 2009.

[26] Whom he misunderstood, according to E. A. Clark 1992:96.

[27] Goldhill 1995:43.

[28] For this question see Averil Cameron 1998.

[29] Sternbach 1892, no. 46, addressed to the "holy" Methodius; see Franchi 2009:79.

[30] See Averil Cameron, forthcoming a.

his bishopric at Cyrrhus, and was condemned by the second Council of Ephesus in 449. Theodoret was also a very different figure—a prominent and very active bishop and a controversial theologian, historian, hagiographer, and writer in many genres. The *Eranistes* makes no pretensions to literary scene-setting. It consists of three exchanges between two speakers, an Orthodoxos and Eranistes ("gatherer", "collector"). Views of the *Eranistes* differ: for Frances Young it "beautifully illustrates the clarity and conciseness of Theodoret's style."[31] Paul Clayton has analysed the theological argument in some detail in relation to Theodoret's position, but with no mention of the work's dialogue form,[32] while Adam Schor, who has recently used it in his study of Theodoret using social network analysis, regards it as outwardly a dialogue, but actually "a vital debate," a Dyophysite apology before the trial of Eutyches and "Theodoret's boldest foray into Christology," written in a period of high controversy and personal crisis for Theodoret.[33] A reviewer of Schor's book took a much dimmer view, admitting that the *Eranistes* is "a good piece" but that many people loathed Theodoret.[34]

The three dialogues that comprise the *Eranistes* are certainly not open. As the text tells us, they are designed to prove respectively that the divine nature of Christ is immutable, that the two natures are unmixed, and that the godhead is impassible. The titles, *Atreptos*, *Asunchutos*, and *Apathes*, pick up the very themes that were the subject of heated debate even before the Council of Ephesus. As we saw, Frances Young offers a sympathetic reading; she points out places where Eranistes is given a more positive role in the argument, especially in the second dialogue (Theodoret "has the skill to use the dialogue form effectively to present both sides of the case"),[35] though Orthodoxos naturally wins in the end. In the third dialogue also, she thinks that "the discussion has not been unfairly presented," and that it shows that an open-minded reader of Theodoret's work could have reached an accommodation. "Perhaps the purpose of the *Eranistes* [after 'twenty years of debate'] was to try and convince the less extreme Alexandrians that they should abandon Eutyches and recognize how much common ground they had with the moderate Antiochenes."[36] In other words the *Eranistes* was less a polemic than a genuine attempt at rapprochement.

However, I am less interested here in the content than the form. Theodoret explains himself in the preface: "the argument will proceed dialogically, with questions and answers, theses and antitheses, and all that is characteristic of

[31] Young 1983:278.
[32] Clayton 2007:chap. 7.
[33] Schor 2011:121, 184–185, 208.
[34] Wickham 2012:337.
[35] Young 1983:281–282.
[36] Young 1983:283.

the dialogue form. However, I will not put the names of the questioners and respondents in the dialogue itself, like the ancient Greek philosophers, but before the beginning of the paragraphs (that is, in the margins [rather like a dramatic script]). For they wrote for people who had every kind of *paideia*, and for whom argument was their life, whereas I want my arguments to be easy to read, and help easy to find, even for those who have no training in argument (*logoi*) ... "The speakers will be called Orthodoxos (the one who argues on behalf of the apostolic dogmas) and Eranistes (the other)."[37] The work may look more like a set of questions and answers,[38] though the latter tend to be more scholastic (*aporiai*) or pastoral; but clearly Theodoret had consciously thought about, and rejected, a more Socratic format.

It will probably seem to most readers that Theodoret here bears out the charge that Christian dialogues had a foregone conclusion. In 449, the year of the *Tome* of Pope Leo, Theodoret was condemned, along with Ibas of Edessa and Domnus of Antioch, by the so-called Robber Council of Ephesus (Ephesus II), which also condemned Flavian of Constantinople and reinstated Eutyches. The condemnation was overturned two years later at Chalcedon in AD 451, after considerable efforts had been made even after a positive move by Pope Leo to establish that Theodoret could be admitted to the Council, but was reasserted by the Council of 553 in Constantinople.[39] Theodoret's doctrinal opponent and target in the *Eranistes* was clearly Eutyches, who proclaimed the one nature of Christ after the union, although the name is never mentioned, and the work as a whole is part of Theodoret's assertion of his own position at a time when Dioscorus, Cyril's successor in Alexandria, favored Eutyches, and when Theodoret was again coming under attack.

The *Eranistes* is not a dialogue of the Platonic type, and most scholars have been unreceptive towards it. It is barely mentioned in the useful introduction to Theodoret's writings in the series The Early Church Fathers, and not included in the selection of texts there;[40] equally it receives only the most passing mentions in a recent study of Theodoret focusing on his role as bishop.[41] Despite what

---

[37] Ettlinger 1975 and 2003:preface. For the practice of placing names in the margins see Wilson 1970:305; Lim 1991:81–82, both discussing Theodoret; Andrieu 1954:part 2, 283–344, especially 304–315. For a precedent among Platonic dialogues, cf. the opening of the *Theaetetus*, 143 b–c, with Ford 2009:34n20, "dropping things like 'I said,' or 'he replied.'" See also Cyril of Alexandria's *Dialogues on the Trinity*, on which see below.

[38] Theodoret knew the difference, and himself produced *Questions* on the Octateuch (Fernandez-Marcos and Saenz-Badillos 1979); the *Questions and Answers to the Orthodox* is a work attributed to Justin Martyr that has been assigned to Theodoret, though scholars are divided on its authorship; see Papadogiannakis 2012:21–22.

[39] Ettlinger 1975:3–4.

[40] Pásztori-Kupán 2006, cf. 20 ("his work against Monophysitism").

[41] Urbainczyk 2002:27, 30.

the author claims, there is no sign that it actually persuaded his theological opponents.

Yet Theodoret was a prolific writer who had probably studied at Antioch and was very well trained not only in Greek rhetoric but also, it seems, in philosophy. Although most of his life was spent in Aramaic-speaking regions he wrote in Greek, not only in his theological works but also in the many letters he wrote in his capacity as a bishop,[42] and while he had more connection with Syriac than has formerly been recognized, his theological, philosophical and rhetorical engagement as shown in his surviving works was with Greek intellectual culture.[43] His apologetic work, the *Cure for Hellenic Maladies*, followed Clement of Alexandria and Eusebius in turning Plato to Christian use.[44] As its preface shows, the *Eranistes* itself is not without literary or intellectual pretensions. According to Richard Lim, the work really was designed to help Theodoret's readers and "favours clarity" over the "ludic free play" of Platonic dialogues.[45] It is indeed interesting that Theodoret should have felt the need to explain his procedure, and also, as Lim says, that he chose the dialogue form. However, we should not take Theodoret's claim of simplicity at face value, and it was a trope he shared with many other Christian writers. Nor is the *Eranistes* best interpreted by being "set alongside" Theodoret's *Historia Religiosa*, as a work supposedly demonstrating the author's wish to insert himself somewhere in the space between those with Greek *paideia* and the uneducated wider Christian population.[46] Rather, it is a product of passion and of personal and intellectual engagement with contemporary and highly technical (and important) doctrinal disputes. It also demonstrates the wide range of dialogue types and their utility in Christian argument.

It appears that Theodoret had much less knowledge of Aristotle than of Plato. This has been held to be common among patristic authors, some of whom criticized the resort to Aristotelian dialectic and syllogisms and professed to associate it with heretics, whom they termed "new Aristotelians."[47] Theodoret professedly stood on the side of those who categorized the employment of Aristotelian dialectic in doctrinal argument as *technologia* rather *theologia*.[48] A further important feature of the *Eranistes* is that each of its three dialogues

---

[42] Azéma 1955–1968, 1982.

[43] Millar 2007; Johnson, forthcoming.

[44] Siniossoglou 2008 is dismissive of Theodoret's knowledge of Plato, but see Papadogiannakis 2012. Papadogiannakis 2012, chapter 5, discusses the literary aspects of Theodoret's writing (though not the *Eranistes*).

[45] Lim 2009:165.

[46] Lim 2009:165–166.

[47] See Elders 1994; Runia 1989; the teaching of Aristotle: Ierodiakonou and Zografidis 2010.

[48] See Lim 1995a:122.

ends with a *florilegium* of patristic citations. The work also has an Appendix, consisting of 40 summaries of the arguments of each dialogue, which is also preserved separately. In his recent book Adam Schor says that the *Eranistes* "intermixed" three genres: dialogue, *florilegia* and "dialectical syllogism."[49] Scholars including the work's editor have taken a remark by Theodoret at the end of his preface to refer to the Appendix: "After the three contests we will add more material, appending a collection (*syllogismos*) to each part." Much later, Byzantine writers of dialogues did frequently draw up lists of syllogisms to support their arguments,[50] but if Theodoret was doing the same this would be a very early example. The most natural interpretation of his words is that he is not using the word *syllogismos* in its technical sense and that he is referring to the *florilegia*. Yet the forty summaries appended to the work as a whole, even if not classic syllogisms in themselves, clearly point forward to the future.

The *florilegia* are important. Like the vanquished Jews in the *Adversus Iudaeos* texts, Eranistes marvels at the discussion and admires Orthodoxos's erudition, whereupon Theodoret gives to Orthodoxos concluding lines likening the selection of proof texts to the activity of bees searching for the right flowers—they often find themselves among dangerous blossoms, but choose the right ones.[51] The key was to produce citations that could be agreed to be unquestionably orthodox, and Theodoret finds no less than 237, even excluding the citations from Leo that were inserted later.[52] Proof texts had been a feature of Christian dialogue since Justin,[53] but doctrinal *florilegia* as such seem to have been a development coinciding with the arguments around the Council of Ephesus in 431, as it became more and more necessary to "prove" rival doctrinal positions.[54] We can see the development represented by Theodoret in terms of the technologizing of Christian doctrinal debate, and with it also of Christian dialogues.[55] Theodoret may already have produced a *florilegium* himself during his earlier arguments against Cyril, but the source of the three *florilegia* accompanying the *Eranistes* is not entirely clear.[56] It has been argued that the *Eranistes* draws on an earlier *florilegium* prepared at the time of the Council of Ephesus, possibly by Theodoret,[57]

---

[49] Schor 2011:184–185.
[50] See Bydén 2004. Bydén connects the cases he discusses with the Byzantine debates with the Latins about the union of the churches, but the phenomenon was considerably wider; see also Aerts 1997:657–658.
[51] *Eranistes*, p. 253; the figure of the bee: Ciccolella 2006.
[52] Clayton 2007:218 with detailed discussion.
[53] See Skarsaune 1987.
[54] Richard 1951 (2011).
[55] "Short proofs" and *florilegia*: Ierodiakonou and Zografidis 2010:856–858, and cf. Uthemann 1981a.
[56] Ettlinger 1975:26.
[57] Theodoret *Letter* 170.

but others derive these *florilegia* from his lost *Pentalogos*, also from soon after 431. The level of Theodoret's own agency in collecting the actual citations is of course an interesting question, though not strictly for the present discussion.

Theodoret was not the first to cast a theological debate in terms of an orthodox versus a heretical speaker. His rival and enemy Cyril of Alexandria (with whom he had exchanged a war of pamphlets before the Council of Ephesus) had himself written seven dialogues on the Trinity and two on Christology, calling the two speakers A and B.[58] Like Theodoret in the *Eranistes*, Cyril explains his technique in a preface to his dialogues on the Trinity,[59] referring to the dialogues as a *logos* consisting of seven *logidia*. Cyril's opponent is Hermias, a man "highly qualified," and the style is "informal," an exchange of questions and answers between two speakers.[60] Interestingly, the word used by Cyril for this conversational style (*aneimene*) is what is prescribed for dialogue, as distinct from rhetoric/oratory and philosophy, in the influential handbook of Demetrius, *On Style*:[61] the style for dialogue should be like that of conversation, that is, simple and informal, as in the opening of Plato's *Republic*, and resembling an extemporary utterance.

Cyril's modern editor clearly found his preface unusual, and comments that Cyril seems to have named real people, yet without the Platonic characterization and scene-setting one might have expected.[62] Cyril's early work, the *De adoratione*, is also a dialogue, or rather a series of dialogues between himself and a certain Palladius on Old Testament exegesis, recently described as having an Atticizing style and (less convincingly) "Platonic" dialogue form.[63] Closer to the *Eranistes*, Cyril's *Thesaurus* drew on writings of Didymus against the Eunomians, which also points to the conclusion that doctrinal dialogue was already in use in the fourth century (seven Ps. Athanasian dialogues survive between an Orthodox and Anomoeans, often attributed to Didymus, though not certainly by him).[64]

The model of short, sharp exchanges between two speakers was also used, for example, in the *Dialogue of Ps. Athanasius and Zacchaeus*, dated to the late fourth

---

[58] Ed. Durand 1976–1978; cf. Durand 1964.

[59] Such prologues are another regular feature, as are metapoetic authorial statements about the chosen literary form and explanations for its use.

[60] Durand 1976–1878:128–129.

[61] *On Style* 19–21, Roberts 1969:78–79; cf. 222–225, p. 64.

[62] Except for the prologue, further attempts at verisimilitude in the seven dialogues on the Trinity are rare, and dialogues III, IV, VI and VII all end with a doxology.

[63] PG 68. 133–1125; see Blackburn Jr. 2009:31; Young 1983:246–248; cf. Young 1997:262–263. Schurig 2005:38 argues against classifying the work as an example of *erotapokriseis*, while according to Blackburn, citing Weber 2000, it is a "didactic dialogue."

[64] PG 28. 1115–1268, 1291–1338; see Heron 1973 (not by Didymus, but late fourth-century).

century in a recent study by Patrick Andrist, though placed in the sixth by Vincent Déroche,[65] and was followed in later centuries, for instance by Anastasius, the late sixth-century patriarch of Antioch, in a dialogue set in Jerusalem between an Orthodox and a Tritheite, which consists of 907 lines of short exchanges followed by a final exposition by Orthodoxos.[66] Like Theodoret, though more briefly, the author explains in the introductory paragraphs that he inserted designations for his speakers for the sake of providing clarity for his readers.[67]

The interest of the *Eranistes* for us as students of Christian dialogue lies in its formalism, its use of the terminology of classification, its use of *florilegia* of proof texts, and its place in the spectrum of anti-heretical literature or heresiology. The *Eranistes* is a complex work, combining several elements that were to be important in the later history of the Christian dialogue form. It perfectly demonstrates the close connection between dialogue, apologetic and polemic that is apparent in the second-century examples, and it also marks a significant step in the formalization of anti-heretical literature. Lists of patristic citations were no idle adornment: they formed part of the proceedings of the Council of Ephesus, and the stakes were high in terms of the future of individuals and groups, including that of Theodoret himself.[68] Richard's work has demonstrated that individual writers drew on core sources in different ways to suit their purpose, and Theodoret cites from heretical sources with the explicit expectation that his opponent will find these more convincing. Establishing the sources of such *florilegia* is usually complex, and the editor of the *Eranistes* argues against earlier theories of a second edition by Theodoret incorporating extracts from the *Tome* of Leo (449), and argues that Theodoret based the *florilegia* on his own earlier work and his own research, the material from the *Tome* being due to later interpolation. But the existence of a complex and extensive manuscript tradition for the *Eranistes* is indicative of its afterlife during the centuries following its composition, and of responses to it that differed markedly from those of modern scholars.

In assessing the development of Christian dialogues and the ways in which they became intertwined with polemical and controversialist literature, we need to look beyond a straightforward comparison with their Platonic and other classical predecessors. Christian dialogues were not innocent literary productions: their purpose was to influence thought, and in many cases also to demonstrate the weakness of opposing arguments, whether those of imaginary Jews, doctrinal rivals or, later, Muslims, and while still casting their own arguments in

---

[65] Andrist 2001; cf. Déroche 1991:276.
[66] See Uthemann 1981b.
[67] Uthemann 1981b: lines 7–8.
[68] Graumann 2009.

dialogue form they used all possible techniques of polemic, classification, proof texts and appeals to authority and hierarchy. It is true, then, that they do not represent open-ended discussion, because, to resort to an over-used cliché, they are about power, or, at least, about the assertion of authority in a highly competitive situation.[69] The issues at stake were real, urgent, and often practical in their application to individuals. An adequate reading of what may seem to us an artificial form of literary production must encompass more than a consideration of the relation of literary dialogues to "real" debate, or to literary and philosophical predecessors and models: it needs to move to an analysis which asks how they formed opinion, how they contributed to the definition of "orthodoxy," and how they acted to establish an approved and accepted mindset. Multiform as these dialogues clearly were, they were nevertheless a tool of opinion-formation, and their rhetorical techniques need to be approached from that perspective. The late Thomas Sizgorich set out some of the rhetorical strategies found in Christian texts in term of "boundary maintenance" and "narratives of identity" between competing groups;[70] as we saw in chapter 2, individuals were equally caught up in this competitive and challenging situation. In this broader enterprise polemic was an essential tool, and polemic infiltrated the supposedly benign and open dialogue form as practiced by Christians from a very early stage.

Many problems surround the understanding of these texts, not least the fact that there is still a fundamental need for more critical editions;[71] for instance, questions of readership and circulation, and the relationship of dialogues with other forms of Christian writing with similar objectives, especially sets of questions and answers.[72] The fictive apocryphal dialogue represents a further extension of the range, including for example the debate with a number of Jews under the auspices of Constantine and Helena in the so-called *Acts of Sylvester*.[73] Another large body of material to be considered is provided by embedded dialogue passages in other texts, especially martyr acts and hagiography. Reported dialogue in council acts is yet another large topic. We have seen already that dialogues could take many forms; the dialogue as a stand-alone literary form is only one of them.

I will end by illustrating the highly complex interplay between historical "evidence," literary and fictional dialogue, and the complications of dating and

---

[69] Averil Cameron 2007, 2012.

[70] Sizgorich 2009: chaps. 1 and 2.

[71] The need is far greater for the Byzantine period.

[72] Jacobs 2007:329, referring to "a space for the dialogic cacophony of different voices even as they were ostensibly refining and narrowing the bounds of 'orthodox' identity"; see above, chapter 1.

[73] The earliest version of this text seems to go back to the fifth or sixth century; it contains a debate, in twelve sessions, between Constantine, his mother Helena, pagan judges and twelve Jewish scholars.

establishing the actual text in question, by considering just one more example, a mysterious dialogue that is part of a wider dossier of texts and that purports to have taken place between Gregentius, archbishop of Taphar (Zafar), the capital of the kingdom of Himyar in southern Arabia, and a learned Jew called Herban.[74] Its dramatic date is the sixth century, evidently before the emergence of Islam, and it provides a mythical account of the Christianization of Himyar under Ethiopian rule, but the text itself is much later, indeed perhaps as much as four centuries later.

Though supposedly set in Himyar, the dialogue opens with a scene-setting frame, saying that it was held at the command of the king (*basileus*) and in the presence of the "senate" and every possible learned man including learned Jews (Scribes and Pharisees) summoned from every city.[75] Though obviously fictional, the dialogue is of interest in the context of the considerable amount of recent scholarship on Himyar and its religious situation in the sixth century, and poses intriguing questions of date and provenance as well as form.[76] The pre-Islamic kingdom of Himyar has attracted the attention of historians for its large numbers of late antique monotheistic inscriptions, its period of Jewish rule, during which fell the so-called "martyrdom" of the Christians of Najran in the early sixth century at the orders of its then Jewish ruler, and its subsequent period of Christian rule from Ethiopia (Axum), with attempts by its ruler Abraha to extend control over other parts of Arabia, before it came under the control of the Sasanians in the 570s.[77] The task is made more difficult by the complexity of the relevant texts, among which our dialogue occupies a peripheral, but undoubtedly intriguing role.

This extremely long work enjoyed a wide circulation, and more than 50 manuscripts are known.[78] Someone evidently thought it worthwhile in the tenth century to compose a lengthy and detailed conspectus of Christian argu-

---

[74] In addition to the *Dialexis* (CPG 7009) the dossier also includes the *Life* of Gregentius and the so-called *Laws of the Himyarites*; all are impressively edited with English translation by A. Berger (Berger 2006). Berger concludes his discussion of the date of composition (Berger 2006:92–107) by arguing that the dialogue dates from the mid-tenth century, and that although written in higher style, it is by the same author as the *Life*, and perhaps written in the Constantinopolitan monastery of Maximina (see Berger 2006:40).

[75] A, lines 1–15, Berger 2006:450. The meeting-place is described as the "Threlleton," probably evokes the Trullanum of the palace at Constantinople and suggests awareness of the Council held there in 691–692: see Déroche 1991:151–152; Berger 2006:94. Berger argues that the dialogue was probably composed in Constantinople (against Shahid 1979 and Olster 1994).

[76] See Fiaccadori 2006.

[77] See Beaucamp et al. 2010; Gajda 2009; Robin 2012; Robin, forthcoming; Bowersock 2012:chap. 1.

[78] Andrist 2000:285; the Greek text was printed with a Latin translation in 1586, paraphrased in Modern Greek in 1646 and translated, and even dramatized, in Turkish in the nineteenth century (Berger 2006:160–162).

ments against Judaism and to give it a fictional setting in South Arabia several centuries earlier; the resulting literary composition found eager readers. The dialogue offers little by way of detail about the historical Himyar. Its conclusion slides further into imaginative hagiography: after lengthy debate, Herban and the Jews challenge Gregentius to show them the resurrected Christ, after which the archbishop withdraws and prays, at which the earth shakes and Christ himself appears in the presence of the king and his notables, surrounded by a purple cloud, and addresses the company, at which the Jews are struck with blindness like Saul on the road to Damascus. Gregentius promises that their sight will be restored if they accept baptism and promptly baptizes one of them as a proof, after which Herban and all the rest are baptized.[79] The king stands as Herban's sponsor, names him Leo and enrols him in the senate, and all Jews in cities everywhere are baptized, a feature which betrays the dialogue's fanciful nature. Gregentius then asks the king to make a law according to which the baptized Jews must marry their sons and daughters to Christians, thereby Christianizing the land of Himyar.[80] With this fairy tale the dialogue ends, with the happy Christianization of Himyar under the blessed Gregentius and his royal patron and the death and burial of Gregentius at Zafar, saying nothing about the historical fate of Himyar under the Sasanians or the eventual arrival of Islam.

One interesting point comes early on, when the Jew laments the fact that the Hebrew Scriptures had ever been translated into "the elaborated language of the Greeks," thus allowing Christians to debate them,[81] for Justinian's *Novel* 146 (AD 553) permitted the use of Greek or other languages in place of Hebrew for the reading of the Scriptures in synagogues, and (grudgingly) allowed the use of the Aquila translation as well as the Septuagint. In another telling note of verisimilitude, which links the dialogue with the *Life*, Herban is said to have noticed notes being taken of the discussion by Palladius, Gregentius's *scholasticus*, whom he had supposedly brought from Alexandria.[82] Gregentius's tone is often scathing and Herban is reduced to silence, and the Jews are astonished, while the king rejoices with the notables at Gregentius's success. He is still present on a third and fourth day, and for the climactic appearance of Christ.

This is a strange and extraordinarily long dialogue, with many features that are unusual in the context of other *Adversus Iudaeos* literature. The dossier in which it is preserved is highly complex and its date and authorship uncertain to say the least. Yet behind it must lie, besides a dim awareness of some historical

---

[79] Berger 2006:E, 480–708, pp. 783–799.

[80] Berger 2006:E, 695–709, p. 798.

[81] Berger 2006:A, 44–45, p. 455. Excellent discussion of the argumentation and structure of the *Dialexis* by Berger 2006:114–134, noting that Herban is "portrayed in quite a vivid manner" (122).

[82] Berger 2006:80.

features of pre-Islamic Himyar, the end of Christian rule there, and perhaps of the wider seventh-century context, a consciousness of the continuing utility of Christian-Jewish dialogue over a period of many centuries and of the imaginative potential and enduring attractiveness of the dialogue form.

In this chapter we have considered three examples (four, if we include the dialogues of Cyril of Alexandria), chosen for their contrasting qualities. There is no typical dialogue, any more than there is a standard Greek term used in manuscripts as the titles of such texts. Yet the dialogue had an extraordinary persistence as a literary form. It was surely its flexibility that made it so popular and gave it such a long life in the Greek east.

Conclusion

The Byzantine Future

I HAVE MADE A CASE HERE for Christian dialogues in late antiquity and beyond as a large and fruitful field of research, over and above comparisons with Socratic or Ciceronian dialogues, and at the same time indicated something of the richness of the available material. Many more dialogues were composed than I have had the space to consider here. Dialogue and debate were everywhere in the late antique world. Despite the efforts of emperors and others, debate did not stop. It was also often passionate, yet even then intense disagreements and rivalries were very often expressed in the literary form of dialogues.

Inevitably, Christian dialogue had a purpose; it was not dialogue for dialogue's sake. But there were differences: if Christians engaged in or wrote about exchanges with Jews, for instance, one can fairly say that there was a foregone conclusion. Sidney Griffith has noted a difference between the harsh language used by Christians against Jews, especially (but not only) in the heightened competitive tensions of seventh-century Palestine,[1] and the more conciliatory tone of Christian-Muslim works written under Islamic rule.[2] This did not apply in the same way to later dialogues between Christians and Muslims written in Byzantium, and the attitude of Christians to Jews, which was at times defensive, but often simply aggressive, was also very different. Intra-Christian debates could be equally sharp; moreover, they took place in a context when deposition, exile or sometimes worse fates could threaten, as well, of course, as the defense of what those involved passionately held to be Christian truth. Much later, complaints about the arrogant and aggressive tone of the Latin participants in the debates about the union of churches are a constant feature in the Byzantine dialogues. Some in late antiquity, Augustine among them, were very aware of the tendency of dialogues to become eristic, and saw this as a danger (though Augustine was no mean controversialist himself). But these dialogues played an important role in forming opinion on matters that were

---

[1] On which, see Averil Cameron 2002a.
[2] Griffith 1992 (2011):272–273.

by no means settled, while even within the wide variety of Christian dialogue material room was at times found for the characteristics of indeterminacy and the dialogic. The *erotapokriseis* in particular make it clear that questions were asked on a wide variety of topics, and such questioning was by no means confined to the question-and-answer literature.[3] The doctrinal content of late antique Christianity was far from fixed. Moreover, despite strong efforts on the part of emperors and church alike, councils continued to be challenged and orthodoxy remained in contention throughout the Byzantine period.[4] The idea that Platonic dialogues themselves were "democratic" is also very much open to question. But Vittorio Hösle is right when he says that in the modern and philosophical senses, genuine dialogue can only flourish if there is mutual respect, and when each side is willing to learn from the other.[5]

The study of dialogue and debate offers a vitally important way of understanding the workings not only of intellectual culture in late antiquity but also of late antique and indeed Byzantine religious culture. Christians did not "resist" dialogue[6] so much as put it to their own uses. Far from ending in the fifth century or thereabouts, as has been so provocatively asserted, the dialogue form was then about to enter one of its most lively periods.

One of the advantages of focusing on the Greek literature of late antiquity is that it allows a connection to be made with literary production in Byzantium; this is especially useful in view of the importance of rhetoric and rhetorical training in Byzantine literature, and the extensive use made of earlier literary and linguistic models.

I have already had occasion to note that Byzantine writers continued to use the prose dialogue form. It was very frequently used for theological subjects, for instance in the Comnenian and Palaeologan periods, even when one might have thought that a straightforward treatise would have been equally appropriate. Dialogues are also a prominent part of the large body of anti-Latin writing, dealing with the *Filioque* and other issues, and contrary to common assumptions, they vary considerably in literary features as well as argument. Some of them claim to be the records of the many actual debates between Byzantines and Latins or Byzantines and Armenians, but as with the late antique examples, this is not always the case, nor are these claims always to be trusted. Moreover, Byzantine writers also wrote prose dialogues on quite different topics and with

---

[3] The extent of such questioning in the late sixth century in relation to the powers of the saints is highlighted by Dal Santo 2012, and see Sarris et al. 2011.

[4] The variety and dynamism of Byzantine and medieval Christianity (or "Christianities") is a main theme in Noble and Smith 2008.

[5] Compare his concluding remarks at Hösle 2012:462–463.

[6] Goldhill 2009:6–7.

varying degrees of Platonizing scene-setting. When for example in the late eleventh century the ecclesiastic and philosopher Eustratius of Nicaea was drawn into a quarrel about the religious status of church treasures, he chose to express his arguments in dialogue form, with a narrative introduction and speakers whose names mean "Lover of truth" and "Lover of custom." Theophylact of Ohrid chose the dialogue form when he wrote on eunuchs, around 1100; the works of Theodore Prodromus in the twelfth century included a philosophical dialogue, the *Xenedemos*, with reference to Porphyry's *Eisagoge*, or introduction to Aristotle's *Categories*; and the intense and competitive literary world of the Palaeologan period produced still more variety in topics, including a prose dialogue between the rich and the poor indicative of contemporary social and economic conditions.

Prose dialogues such as these, and many others, are part not only of the history of Byzantine literature but also of Byzantine philosophy, a topic that is receiving renewed attention.[7] In particular, the history of Platonic reception in Byzantium is complex. Some Byzantines, at certain periods, were very well versed in Plato, and some dialogue writers were sufficiently aware of a limited range of Platonic models to use them in the narrative settings of their own works. A well-known and large group of Byzantine Greek manuscripts testifies to the copying in the late ninth century and later of an extensive group of Neoplatonic and Aristotelian texts, together with some Christian authors who include Maximus Confessor and John of Damascus.[8] However, except in their number and variety, Plato's dialogues themselves occupy a minor place in comparison with works deriving from Alexandrian Neoplatonism or late Aristotelianism,[9] although a small number of key manuscripts deriving from this period have guaranteed their preservation.[10] The number of manuscripts of Aristotle is overwhelming by comparison. The name of Plato also came to be used, especially in the eleventh century and later, as shorthand for dangerous "Hellenic" (that is, pagan) doctrines, and the suspicion of enthusiasm for the content of his work, as opposed to its value for instruction, could be extremely dangerous. Plato enjoyed something of a return in the late Byzantine period, especially in the work of George Gemistus Plethon,[11] although this was (probably not surprisingly) accompanied by a return of interest in debating the rival merits of Plato and Aristotle. Most important from our present point of view is the fact that

---

[7] Ierodiakonou 2002; Bydén and Ierodiakonou 2012.
[8] See Ronconi 2012 for the very complex issues surrounding this manuscript tradition; a survey of the troubled reception of Plato in Byzantium can be found in Tambrun-Krasker 2012.
[9] Ronconi 2012:156.
[10] See Tambrun-Krasker 2012:7–8 for the interesting later history of Par. gr. 1807 and Clarkianus 39.
[11] Tambrun-Krasker 2006; Siniossoglou 2008.

unlike the logical works of Aristotle, Plato's dialogues were not a regular part of the standard Byzantine educational system, which remained weighted towards rhetoric, and in which Aristotle's logical works were one of the main platforms. This situation, we may add, leaves wide open many questions about the literary analysis of Greek dialogues from all parts of the Byzantine period, and surely also explains the very limited range of Platonic dialogues whose influence is perceptible. If anything, it makes it all the more mysterious that "Platonic" dialogue continued at all, in however attenuated a literary form.

Both the philosophical and the literary histories of Byzantium are complex, and each is currently the subject of radical rethinking among revisionist scholars.[12] Yet dialogues did continue to be written, albeit at some periods more than others, and even if the subject has been rarely as yet studied by literary scholars. It is an indication of the general lack of attention to Byzantium by others that neither the dialogues just mentioned, or the many other Byzantine examples of prose dialogues, find any place in Hösle's book.[13]

Classicists and late antique scholars have usually been reluctant to venture forward into Byzantium, partly for fear of assuming a specious continuity, but mainly because of an inherited dismissal of Byzantium and Byzantine culture.[14] The ideologically fraught associations of any assertion of continuity have in turn impeded many Byzantinists from serious consideration either of Greek imperial literature or of the literature of late antiquity, except to describe certain works and writers as "early Byzantine." This situation obscures some important questions, especially in relation to literary production in the centuries from, say, the fourth to the ninth. In addition, the lengthening of late antiquity that is currently in vogue has the effect of obscuring Byzantium, while the increasing focus in current late antique scholarship on the east and on literature in east Christian languages tends in a similar direction.[15] It is true that this book takes dialogues in late antiquity, and not Byzantium, as its subject; but a further challenge remains, that of bringing these late antique dialogues together in a critical way with the huge amount of material from Byzantium.[16] It would surely be worth attempting such an approach.

---

[12] Averil Cameron, forthcoming b.

[13] Even the otherwise excellent article by Tannous takes as a starting point the assumption of "the withering away of certain traditional genres of Greek literature ... seen as one of the most notable characteristics of the so-called Byzantine 'Dark Ages'": Tannous 2013:83.

[14] Averil Cameron, forthcoming b: chap. 1.

[15] Johnson, forthcoming, offers a welcome counter-balance, but his remit does not allow him to include the literary history of Constantinople and the Byzantine empire as such.

[16] Odorico 2012 is a very good example of some of the approaches now being taken among scholars of Byzantine literature; in particular, Bianconi 2012 marks a distinct advance in considering the audiences and contexts of controversy literature in late Byzantium, even if not of dialogues as

If in this book I have taken a generous definition of dialogue—some might say too generous—that is because I believe this to be necessary if we are to grasp either the amount or the variety of material that would be involved in a full study. One of the questions that will need to be addressed in the future concerns the apparent difference between the more literary dialogues and those that seem more utilitarian, or more like disputations, with long speeches rather than interchanges. I believe it is premature, however, to apply such a distinction at this stage in the inquiry, and we are certainly not helped by the multitude of terms in use in the sources and in manuscripts, or by the tendency of modern scholars to adopt such titles uncritically, or, as is common practice, to apply Latin titles to Greek works.

We ourselves live in an age when "dialogue" means something quite different from what it meant to the authors discussed in here. We are exhorted to talk and reach common solutions, as in a recent article in the *New York Review of Books* headed "Why we must talk" (that is, talk rather than fight). The ideal of consensus based on mutual agreement through controlled discussion is deeply rooted in contemporary political life, and the word "dialogue" appears constantly in general usage. We are taught to value discussion, mediation and consensus, and many organizations exist to promote dialogue and to train people in its techniques, as well as journals devoted to dialogue studies. Inter-faith agendas are apparent in modern studies of Christian-Jewish and Christian-Muslim dialogues, and they also promote dialogue in contemporary life: a "Dialogue Society," with branches in Oxford and elsewhere,[17] exists, as its publicity states, to further social cohesion by facilitating dialogue, especially between Muslims and Christians. It advertises training and help in dialogue skills—cultivating empathy and effective listening—with ten-week placements for masters' students. Goldhill is right when he says that "modern Christians" (and others) find the repressive tone of many late antique Christian dialogues unattractive. But we must be careful about applying our own criteria of what does and does not count as "real" dialogue. In fact late antiquity was an age of dialogue and debate *par excellence*. As a tool for the student of religion, of the concept of orthodoxy and of the intellectual culture of late antiquity and Byzantium, the importance of the dialogues composed by Christian writers in late antiquity, and of the actual debates that took place, is truly fundamental.

---

such, while Messis 2012 offers a highly contextual reading of Theophylact of Ohrid's so-called *Apology for Eunuchs*.

[17] Founded in 1999 in London along the principles of the Turkish Gülen movement.

Bibliography

Editions and Translations of Primary Sources

Allen, P. 2009. *Sophronius of Jerusalem and Seventh-Century Heresy: The Synodical Letter and Other Documents; Introduction, Texts, Translations and Commentary.* Oxford.

Allen, P., and B. Neil. 1999. *Scripta Saeculi VII Vitam Maximi Confessoris Illustrantia.* Corpus Christianorum, Series Graeca 39. Turnhout.

———. 2002. *Maximus the Confessor and his Companions. Documents from Exile.* Oxford.

Azéma, Y. 1955–1968, 1982. *Théodoret de Cyr. Correspondance.* Paris.

Bausenhart, G. 1992. "In allem uns gleich außer der Sünde." In *Studien zum Beitrag Maximos der Bekenner zu altkirchlichen Christologie.* Mainz. German translation of Maximus' debate with Pyrrhus at 196–235, notes at 236–316.

Beeson, C. H. 1906. *Hegemonius. Acta Archelai.* Leipzig.

Bell, P. N. 2009. *Three Political Voices from the Age of Justinian: Agapetus, "Advice to the Emperor": Dialogue on Political Science"; Paul the Silentiary, "Description of Hagia Sophia."* Translated Texts for Historians 52. Liverpool.

Berger, A. 2006. *Life and Works of Saint Gregentios, Archbishop of Taphar: Introduction, Critical Edition and Translation.* Berlin.

Bobichon, P. 2003. *Justin Martyr. Dialogue avec Trypho.* 2 vols. Fribourg.

Bonwetsch, E. 1891. *Methodius von Olympus.* Erlangen.

Bratke, E. 1899. *Das sogennante Religionsgespräch am Hof der Sasaniden.* Leipzig.

Brock, S., and B. FitzGerald. 2013. *Two Early Lives of Severos, Patriarch of Antioch.* Translated Texts for Historians 59. Liverpool.

Brooks, E. W. 1923–1925. *John of Ephesus. The Lives of the Eastern Saints.* 3 vols. Paris

Colonna, M. E. 1958. *Aeneas of Gaza, Theophrastus sive de immortalitate animae.* Naples.

Courtonne, Y. 1961. *Saint Basile, Lettres II.* Paris.

Daly, R. J. 1992. *Origen. Treatise on the Passover and Dialogue of Origen with Heraclides and his Fellow Bishops on the Father, the Son and the Soul.* Ancient Christian Writers 54. New York.

Dillon, J. M., and W. Polleichtner. 2010. *Iamblichus of Chalcis, The Letters.* Leiden.

Doucet, M. 1972. *Dispute de Maxime le Confesseur avec Pyrrhus, texte critique, traduction et notes*. PhD diss., Université de Montréal, Institut d'Etudes Mediévales. Montreal.

Drijvers, H. J. W. 2006. *The Book of the Laws of Countries: Dialogue on Fate of Bardaisan of Edessa*. Piscataway, NJ.

Dunn, Geoffrey D. 2004. *Tertullian*. London.

Durand, G. M. de. 1964. *Cyrille d'Alexandrie, Deux dialogues christologiques*. Sources chrétiennes 97. Paris.

———. 1976–1978. *Cyrille d'Alexandrie, Dialogues sur la Trinité*. Sources chrétiennes 231, 237, 246. Paris.

Ettlinger, G. H. 1975. *Theodoret, Eranistes*. Oxford.

———. 2003. *Theodoret of Cyrrhus*. Fathers of the Church 106. Washington, DC.

Fernandez-Marcos, N. and A. Saenz-Badillos. 1979. *Theodoreti Cyrensis, Quaestiones in Octateuchum*. Madrid.

Festugière, A. 1961. *Historia monachorum in Aegypto*. Brussels.

Garton, C., and L. G. Westerink. 1978. *Theophylactus Simocates, On Predestined Terms of Life*. Buffalo, NY.

———. 1979. *Germanos on Predestined Terms of Life*. Buffalo, NY.

Gertz, S. et al. 2012. *Aeneas of Gaza, "Theophrastus," with Zacharias of Mytilene, "Ammonius."* London.

Grégoire, H., and M.-A. Kugener. 1930. *Mark the Deacon, Vie de Porphyre évêque de Gaza*. Paris.

Lamberz, E. 2008. *Concilium universale Nicaenum secundum concilii actiones*. Acta Conciliorum Oecumenicorum 2.3. Berlin.

Maas, M., and E. G. Matthews, Jr. 2003. *Exegesis and Empire in the Early Byzantine Mediterranean: Junillus Africanus and the Instituta Regularia Divinae Legis*. Tübingen.

Minniti Colonna, M. E. 1973. *Zacaria Scolastico, Ammonio: Introduzione, Testo Critico, Traduzione, Commentario*. Naples.

Minns, D., and P. Parvis. 2009. *Justin, Philosopher and Martyr: Apologies*. Oxford.

Musurillo, H. 1958. *The Symposium: A Treatise on Chastity*. Westminster, MD.

Musurillo, H., and V.-H. Debidour. 1963. *Méthode d'Olympe, Le Banquet*. Sources chrétiennes 95. Paris.

Pásztori-Kupán, I. 2006. *Theodoret of Cyrus*. London.

Price, R. M. 2009. *The Acts of Constantinople 553, with Related Texts on the Three Chapters Controversy*. Translated Texts for Historians 51. 2 vols. Liverpool.

Price, R. M., and M. Gaddis. 2005. *The Acts of the Council of Chalcedon*. Translated Texts for Historians 45. Liverpool.

Ramelli, I. 2009a. *Bardesane di Edessa, Contro il fato = Kata heimarmenes (detto anche Liber Legum Regionum.* Rome. (For Ramelli 2009b, see below, Secondary Literature.)

Riedinger, R. 1989. *Pseudo-Kaisarios, Die Erotapokriseis.* Berlin.

Roberts, W. R. 1969. *Demetrius on Style: The Greek Text of Demetrius' "De elocutione."* Hildesheim. Orig. pub. Cambridge, 1902.

Roth, P. 1993. *Gregory of Nyssa, De anima et resurrectione.* Crestwood, NY.

Rucker, I. 1933. *Florilegium Edessenum anonymum (Syriace ante 562).* Munich.

Scherer, J. 1960. *Entretien d'Origène avec Héraclide.* Sources chrétiennes 67. Paris.

Sternbach, L. 1892. "Georgii Pisidae, Carmina inedita." *Wiener Studien* 14:51–68.

Trompf, G. W. 1997. *Adamantius, Dialogue on the True Faith in God.* Trans. R. A. Pretty. Leuven.

Van den Ven, P. 1962–1970. *La vie ancienne de S. Syméon Stylite le Jeune, 521–592.* 2 vols. Brussels.

Varner, W. 2005. *Ancient Jewish Dialogues: Athanasius and Zacchaeus, Simon and Theophilus, Timothy and Aquila.* Lewiston, NY.

Whitby, Michael, and Mary Whitby. 1986. *The History of Theophylact Simocatta.* Oxford.

Secondary Literature

Aerts, W. 1997. "Panorama der byzantinischen Literatur." In Engels and Hoffmann 1997, 635–716.

Alexakis, A. 1996. *Codex Parisinus Graecus 1115 and its Archetype.* Washington, DC.

Amato, E. 2010. *Rose di Gaza: Gli scritti retorico-sofistici e le "Epistole" di Procopio di Gaza.* Alexandria.

Amato, E. et al., eds. 2006. *Approches de la Troisième Sophistique: Hommages à Jacques Schamp.* Brussels.

Amirav, H., and R. B. ter Haar Romeny, eds. 2007. *From Rome to Constantinople: Studies in Honour of Averil Cameron.* Leuven.

Ando, C. 1996. "Pagan Apologetics and Christian Intolerance in the Ages of Themistius and Constantine." *Journal of Early Christian Studies* 4:171–207.

Andrieu, J. 1954. *Le dialogue antique: Structure et présentation.* Paris.

Andrist, P. 2000. "Pour un répertoire des manuscrits de polémique antijudaïque." *Byzantion* 70:270–306.

———. 2001. *Le "Dialogue d'Athanase et Zachée": Étude des sources et du contexte littéraire.* 2 vols. PhD diss., University of Geneva.

Angold, M., ed. 1984. *The Byzantine Aristocracy.* Oxford.

Ayres, L. 2006. "Introduction." In "The Question of Orthodoxy." Special issue, *Journal of Early Christiian Studies* 14:395–398.

Athanassiadi, P. 2010. *Vers la pensée unique: La montée de l'intolérance dans l'Antiquité tardive.* Paris.

Baker-Brian, N. 2009. *Manichaeism in the Later Roman Empire: A Study of Augustine's Contra Adimantum.* Lewiston, NY.

Bakhtin, M. 1981. *The Dialogic Imagination: Four Essays.* Ed. M. Holquist. Trans. C. Emerson and M. Holquist. Austin.

Bardy, G. 1957. "Dialog (christlich)." In *Reallexikon für Antike und Christentum* III:945–955.

Beatrice, P. F. 1983. "Dialogo." In *Dizionario patristico e di antichità cristiane,* ed. A. di Berardino. 3 vols, 1.939–942.

Beaucamp, J. et al., eds. 2010. *Juifs et chrétiens en Arabie aux Ve et VIe siècles: Regards croisés sur les sources.* Collège de France-CNRS, Centre de recherche d'histoire et civilisation de Byzance Monographies 32, *Le massacre de Najran II.* Paris.

Becker, A. H. 2006. *Fear of God and the Beginning of Wisdom: The School of Nisibis and the Development of Scholastic Culture in Late Antique Mesopotamia.* Philadelphia.

Bedouelle, G., and O. Fatio, eds. 1994. *Liberté chrétienne et libre arbiter.* Fribourg.

Bell, Peter N. 2013. *Social Conflict in the Age of Justinian.* Oxford.

Bennett, Byard. 2003. "Paul the Persian." In *Encyclopaedia Iranica.* Center for Iranian Studies, Columbia University. http://www.iranicaonline.org/articles/paul-the-persian. Accessed November 10, 2013.

Bianconi, D. 2012. "Dire e contraddire: Commitenti, autori e pubblico nella letteratura delle controversie religiose (due esempi dal XIV secolo)." In Odorico 2012:23–40.

Blackburn Jr., B. Lee. 2009. *The Mystery of the Synagogue: Cyril of Alexandria on the Law of Moses.* PhD diss., University of Notre Dame.

Blaudeau, P. 2006. *Alexandrie et Constantinople, 451–491: De l'histoire à la géo-ecclésiologie.* Rome.

Bonfil, R. et al., eds. 2012. *Jews in Byzantium: Dialectics of Minority and Majority Cultures.* Leiden.

Booth, P. 2013. *Crisis of Empire: Doctrine and Dissent at the End of Late Antiquity.* Berkeley.

Bosch-Veciana, A., and Montserrat-Molas, J., eds. 2007. *Philosophy and Dialogue: Studies on Plato's Dialogues* I. Barcelona.

Bowersock, G. W. 1990. *Hellenism in Late Antiquity.* Cambridge.

———. 2012. *Empires in Collision in Late Antiquity.* The Menahem Stern Jerusalem Lectures 2011. Waltham, MA.

Boyarin, D. 2009a. "Dialectic and Divination in the Talmud." In Goldhill 2009:217–241.

———. 2009b. *Socrates and the Fat Rabbis*. Chicago.

Bracht, K. 1999. *Vollkommenheit und Vollendung: Zur Anthropologie des Methodius von Olympos*. Tübingen.

———. 2011. "Methodius von Olympus." *Reallexikon für Antike und Christentum* 25:768–784.

Brakke, D. et al., eds. 2005. *Religion and the Self in Late Antiquity*. Bloomington.

Bril, A. 2005. "Plato and the Sympotic Form in the *Symposium* of St. Methodius of Olympus." *Zeitschrift für antikes Christentum* 9:279–302.

Brock, S. P. 1981. "The Conversations with the Syrian Orthodox under Justinian (532)." *Orientalia Christiana Periodica* 47:87–121.

———. 1984. "Syriac Dialogue Poems: Marginalia to a Recent Edition." *Le Muséon* 97.1–2:29–58.

———. 1987. "Dramatic Dialogue Poems." In Drijvers and Watt 1987:135–147.

———. 1991. "Syriac Dispute Poems: The Various Types." In Reinink and Vanstiphout 1991:109–119.

Brown, P. et al., eds. 1999. *Late Antiquity: A Guide to the Post-Classical World*. Cambridge, MA.

Bryder, P., ed. 1988. *Manichaean Studies* I. Lund.

Buchheit, V. 1958. *Studien zu Methodios von Olympos*. Berlin.

Burrus, V. 2000. *"Begotten, Not Made": Conceiving Manhood in Late Antiquity*. Stanford.

Burrus, V. et al. 2005. Review-discussion of Clark 2004. *Church History* 74:812–836.

Bussières, M.-P. ed. 2013. *La littérature des questions et réponses dans l'Antiquité profane et chrétienne: De l'enseignement à l'exégèse; actes du séminaire sur le genre des questions et réponses tenu à Ottawa les 27 et 28 septembre 2009*. Instrumenta Patristica et Mediaevalia 64. Turnhout.

Bydén, B. 2004. "'Strangle Them with the Meshes of Syllogisms!' Latin Philosophy in Greek Translations of the Thirteenth Century." In Rosenqvist 2004:133–157.

———. 2012. "A Case for Creationism: Christian Cosmology in the 5th and 6th Centuries." In Bydén and Ierodiakonou 2012:79–107.

Bydén, B., and I. Ierodiakonou, eds. 2012. *The Many Faces of Byzantine Philosophy*. Athens.

Cameron, Alan et al. 1977. *Christianisme et formes littéraires de l'antiquité tardive en Occident: Huit exposés suivis de discussions*. Entretiens sur l'antiquité classique 23. Geneva.

Cameron, Averil. 1991a. "Disputations, Polemical Literature and the Formation of Opinion in the Early Byzantine Period." In Reinink and Vanstiphout 1991:91–108.

————. 1991b. *Christianity and the Rhetoric of Empire: The Development of Christian Discourse.* Berkeley.

————. 1995. "Ascetic Closure and the End of Antiquity." In Wimbush and Valantasis 1995:147–161.

————. 1998. "Education and Literary Culture, AD 337–425." In *The Cambridge Ancient History* XIII, ed. Averil Cameron and P. Garnsey, 665–707. Cambridge.

————. 2002a. "Apologetics in the Roman Empire: A Genre of Intolerance?" In Carrié and Testa 2002:219–227.

————. 2002b. "Blaming the Jews: The Seventh-Century Invasions of Palestine in Context." In *Mélanges Gilbert Dagron*, Travaux et mémoires 14, eds. G. Dagron and V. Déroche, 57–78. Paris.

————. 2003. "How to Read Heresiology." *Journal of Medieval and Early Modern Studies* 33.3:471–492. Repr. in Martin and Miller 2005:193–212.

————. 2007. "Enforcing Orthodoxy in Byzantium." In Cooper and Gregory 2007:1–24.

————. 2008a. "The Violence of Orthodoxy." In Iricinschi and Zellentin 2008:102–114.

————. 2008b. "Byzantium and the Limits of Orthodoxy." Raleigh Lecture in History. *Proceedings of the British Academy* 154:139–152.

————. 2012. "The Cost of Orthodoxy." Second Dutch Annual Lecture in Patristics 2011. Leiden. Repr. *Church History and Religious Culture* 93.3 (2013): 339–361.

————. 2013. "Can Christians Do Dialogue?" *Studia Patristica* 63.11:103–120.

————. Forthcoming a. "Culture Wars: Late Antiquity and Literature." In Freu and Janniard, forthcoming.

————. Forthcoming b. *Byzantine Matters.* Princeton.

————. Forthcoming c. *Dialog und Streitgespräch in der Spätantike.* Munich.

Cameron, Averil, and R. G. Hoyland, eds. 2011. *Doctrine and Debate in the East Christian World, 300–1500.* Worlds of Eastern Christianity 300–1500, 12. Farnham.

Cancik, H. 2008. "Antike Religionsgesprache." In Schörner and Sterbenc 2008:15–25.

Cancik, H., and H. Schneider, eds. 2002. *Brill's New Pauly: Encyclopaedia of the Ancient World* IV. Leiden.

Cardelle de Hartmann, C. 2007. *Lateinische Dialoge 1200–1400: Literaturhistorische Studie und Repertorium.* Mittellateinische Studien und Texte 37. Leiden.

Carrié, J.-M., and R. L. Testa, eds. 2002. *"Humana sapit": Études d'antiquité tardive offertes à Lellia Cracco Ruggini.* Bibliothèque de l'Antiquité Tardive 3. Turnhout.

Chrysostomides, J., ed. 1988. *Kathegetria: Essays Presented to Joan Hussey for her 80th Birthday.* Camberley.

Ciccolella, F. 2006. "'Swarms of the Wise Bee': Literati and Their Audience in Sixth-Century Gaza." In Amato et al. 2006: 80–95.

Clark, E. A. 1992. *The Origenist Controversy: The Cultural Construction of an Early Christian Debate.* Princeton.

——. 1995. "Antifamilial Tendencies in Ancient Christianity." *Journal of the History of Sexuality* 5.3:356–380.

——. 1998. "Holy Women, Holy Words: Early Christian Women, Social History and the 'Linguistic Turn.'" *Journal of Early Christian Studies* 6:413–430.

——. 1999. *Reading Renunciation: Asceticism and Scripture in Early Christianity.* Princeton.

——. 2004. *History, Theory, Text: Historians and the Linguistic Turn.* Cambridge, MA.

——. 2008a. "From Patristics to Early Christian Studies." In Harvey and Hunter 2008:7–41.

——. 2008b. "The Celibate Bridegroom and His Virginal Brides: Metaphor and the Marriage of Jesus in Early Christian Ascetic Exegesis." *Church History* 77.1: 1–25.

——. 2009. "Early Christian Asceticism and Nineteenth-Century Polemics." *Journal of Early Christian Studies* 17.2: 281–307.

Clark, G. 2009. "Can We Talk? Augustine and the Possibility of Dialogue." In Goldhill 2009:117–134.

Clayton, P. B., Jr. 2007. *The Christology of Theodoret of Cyrrhus: Antiochene Christology from the Council of Ephesus (431) to the Council of Chalcedon (451).* Oxford.

Cooper, K., and J. Gregory, eds. 2007. *Discipline and Diversity: Papers Read at the 2005 Summer Meeting and the 2006 Winter Meeting of the Ecclesiastical History Society.* Studies in Church History 43. Woodbridge.

Côté, D. 2001a. "La fonction littéraire de Simon le Magicien dans les Pseudo-Clémentines." *Laval théologique et philosophique* 57.3:513–523.

——. 2001b. *Le thème de l'opposition entre Pierre et Simon dans les Pseudo-Clémentines.* Paris.

Cribiore, R. 2001. *Gymnastics of the Mind: Greek Education in Hellenistic and Roman Egypt.* Princeton.

Cubitt, C. 2009. "The Lateran Council of 649 as an Ecumenical Council." In Price and Whitby 2009:133–147.

Cunningham, M. B. 2003. "Dramatic Device or Didactic Tool? The Function of Dialogue in Byzantine Preaching." In Jeffreys 2003:101–113.

Dal Santo, M. 2012. *Debating the Saints' Cults in the Age of Gregory the Great.* Oxford.

D'Costa, G., ed. 1990. *Christian Uniqueness Reconsidered: The Myth of a Pluralistic Theology of Religions.* Maryknoll, NY.

De Bruyn, T. S. 1993. "Ambivalence within a 'Totalizing Discourse': Augustine's Sermons on the Sack of Rome." *Journal of Early Christian Studies* 1.4:404–421.

Déroche, V. 1991. "La polémique anti-judaïque au VIème et VIIème siècle: Un mémento inédit; Les Képhalaia." *Travaux et Mémoires* 11:275–311.

Derda, T. et al. 2007. *Alexandria: Auditoria of Kom el-Dikka and Late Antique Education.* Warsaw.

Di Berardino, A. 1983. *Dizionario Patristico e di Antichità Cristiane* I. Rome.

Dijkstra, J., and G. Fisher, eds. Forthcoming. *Inside and Out: Interactions between Rome and the Peoples on the Arabian and Egyptian Frontiers in Late Antiquity (200-800 CE).* Leuven.

Döpp, S., and W. Geerlings, eds. 2000. *Dictionary of Early Christian Literature.* Trans. M. O'Connell. New York.

Döring, K. 2011. "The Students of Socrates." In Morrison 2011:24–47.

Drake, H. A. 2000. *Constantine and the Bishops: The Politics of Intolerance.* Baltimore, MD.

Drijvers, J. D., and J. Watt, eds. 1999. *Portraits of Spiritual Authority: Religious Power in Early Christianity, Byzantium and the Christian Orient.* Leiden.

Drijvers, H. J. W. 1966. *Bardaisan of Edessa.* Assen.

———. 1994. "Bardaisan's Doctrine of Free Will, the Pseudo-Clementines, and Marcionism in Syria." In Bedouelle and Fatio 1994:13–30.

Drijvers, H. J. W. et al, eds. 1987. *IV Symposium Syriacum 1984: Literary Genres in Syriac Literature.* Rome.

Edwards, M. J. 1991. "On the Platonic Schooling of Justin Martyr." *Journal of Theological Studies* 42: 17–34.

———. 2009. *Catholicity and Heresy in the Early Church.* Farnham.

Edwards, M. J. et al., eds. 1999. *Apologetics in the Roman Empire: Pagans, Jews and Christians.* Oxford.

Elders, L. J. 1994. "The Greek Christian Authors and Aristotle." In Schrenk 1994:111–142.

Elm, S. et al., eds. 2000. *Orthodoxie, christianisme, histoire.* Collection de l'École Française de Rome 270. Paris.

Engels, D., and P. Van Nuffelen, eds. 2014. *Competition and Religion in Antiquity.* Brussels.

Engels, L. J., and H. Hoffmann, eds. 1997. *Spätantike: Mit einem Panorama der byzantinischen Literatur.* Neues Handbuch der Literaturwissenschaft 4. Wiesbaden.

Eshleman, K. 2012. *The Social World of Intellectuals in the Roman Empire: Sophists, Philosophers and Christians.* Cambridge.

Fiaccadori, G. 2006. "Gregentios in the Land of the Homerites." In Berger 2006:48–82.

Flower, R. 2013. *Emperors and Bishops in Fourth-Century Invective.* Cambridge.

Fontaine, J. 1968. *Aspects et problèmes de la prose d'art latine au III siècle: La genèse des types latins chrétiens.* Turin.

———. 1988. "Comment doit-on appliquer la notion du genre littéraire à la littérature latine chrétienne du IV siècle?" *Philologus* 132:53–73.

Ford, A. 2009. "The Beginnings of Dialogue: Socratic Discourse and Fourth-Century Prose." In Goldhill 2009:29–44.

Formisano, M. 2007. "Towards an Aesthetic Paradigm of Late Antiquity." *Antiquité Tardive* 15:277–284.

Franchi, R. 2009. "Il mare in tempesta nel 'De autexousio' di Metodio d'Olimpo e nell' 'Hexaemeron' di Giorgio di Pisidia." *Byzantinische Zeitschrift* 102:65–82.

Frank, G. 2005. "Dialogue and Deliberation: The Sensory Self in the Hymns of Romanos the Melodist." In Brakke et al. 2005:163–179.

Frederiksen, P., and O. Irshai. 2008. "Christian Anti-Judaism: Polemics and Policies." In Katz 2008:977–1034.

Frendo, J. D. C. 1988. "History and Panegyric in the Age of Heraclius: The Literary Background to the Composition of the 'Histories' of Theophylact Simocatta." *Dumbarton Oaks Papers* 42:143–156.

Freu, C., and S. Janniard, eds. Forthcoming. *Mélanges Carrié.* Bibliothèque de l'Antiquité Tardive. Paris.

Führer, T. 2012. "Conversationalist and Consultant: Augustine in Dialogue." In Vessey 2012:270–283.

Gajda, I. 2009. *Le royaume de Himyar à l'époque monothéiste.* Paris.

Gardner, G., and K. L. Osterloh. 2008. *Antiquity in Antiquity: Jewish and Christian Pasts in the Greco-Roman World.* Tübingen.

Garzya, A. 1981. "Testi literari d'uso strumentali." *Jahrbuch der Österreichischen Byzantinistik* 31:263–287.

———, ed. 2006. *Spirito e forma della letteratura bizantina: Actes de la séance plénière d'ouverture du XXe Congrès international des études byzantines (Paris, 2001, 19-25 août).* Naples.

Gerson, L. P., ed. 2010. *The Cambridge History of Philosophy in Late Antiquity.* 2 vols. Cambridge.

Goldhill, S. 1995. *Foucault's Virginity: Ancient Erotic Fiction and the History of Sexuality.* Cambridge.

———, ed. 2009. *The End of Dialogue in Antiquity.* Cambridge.

Goldlust, B. 2010. *Rhétorique et poétique de Macrobe dans les "Saturnales."* Recherches sur les rhétoriques religieuses 14. Turnhout.

Graumann, T. 2009. "'Reading' the First Council of Ephesus (431)." In Price and Whitby 2009:27–44.

Griffith, S. H. 1992 "Disputes with Muslims in Syriac Christian Texts: From Patriarch John (d. 648) to Bar Hebraeus (d. 1286)." In Lewis and Niewöhner 1992: 251–273. Reprinted in Cameron and Hoyland 2011: chap. 6.

———. 2008. *The Church in the Shadow of the Mosque: Christians and Muslims in the World of Islam.* Princeton.

Grillmeier, A., and H. Bacht, eds. 1951. *Das Konzil von Chalkedon* I. Würzburg.

Gronewald, M. 1991. "Palladius, Dialogus de vita S. Ioannis Chrysostomi in P.Ryl. III 508." *Zeitschrift für Papyrologie und Epigraphik* 89:33–34.

Grünbart, M., ed. 2007. *Theatron: Rhetorische Kultur im Spätantike und Mittelalter.* Millenium Studies 13. Berlin.

Guillaumont, A. 1969–1970. "Justinien et l'église de Perse." *Dumbarton Oaks Papers* 23–24:41–66.

———. 1970. "Un colloque entre orthodoxes et théologiens nestoriens de Perse sous Justinien." *Comptes rendus de l'Academie des inscriptions et belles-lettres* 114:201–207.

Gwynn, D. M., and S. Bangert, eds. 2010. *Religious Diversity in Late Antiquity.* Leiden.

Hart, R. and V. Tejera, eds. 1997. *Plato's Dialogues: The Dialogical Approach.* Lewiston, NY.

Harvey, S. A., 2005. "Revisiting the Daughters of the Covenant: Women's Choirs and Sacred Song in Ancient Syriac Christianity." *Hugoye: Journal of Syriac Studies* 8.2:125–149.

Harvey, S. A., and D. Hunter, eds. 2008. *Oxford Handbook of Early Christian Studies.* Oxford.

Heath, M. 2004. *Menander: A Rhetor in Context.* Oxford.

Hempfer, W., ed. 2002. *Möglichkeiten des Dialogs: Struktur und Funktion einer literarischen Gattung zwischen Mittelalter und Renaissance in Italien.* Stuttgart.

Heron, A. 1973. "The Two Pseudo-Athanasian Dialogues against the Anomoeans." *Journal of Theological Studies* 24:101–122.

Heyden, K. 2009. *Die "Erzählung des Aphroditian": Thema und Variationen einer Legende im Spannungsfeld von Christentum und Heidentum.* Tübingen.

Hick, J., and P. F. Knitter, eds. 1987. *The Myth of Christian Uniqueness: Toward a Pluralistic Theology of Religions.* Maryknoll, NY.

Hirzel, R. 1895. *Der Dialog.* 2 vols. Hildesheim.

Hoffmann, M. 1996. *Der Dialog bei den christlichen Schriftstellern der ersten vier Jahrhunderte.* Berlin.

Honnacker, H. 2002. *Der literarische Dialog des Primo Cinquecento: Inszenierungsstrategien und "Spielraum."* Saecula Spiritalia 40. Baden-Baden.

Hopkins, K. A. 1999. *A World Full of Gods: Pagans, Jews and Christians in the Roman Empire.* London.

Horner, T. J. 1999. *Listening to Trypho: Justin Martyr's Dialogue Reconsidered.* Leuven.

Hösle, V. 2012. *The Philosophical Dialogue: A Poetics and Hermeneutics.* Trans. S. Rendall. Notre Dame, IN. Orig. pub. as *Der philosophische Dialog: Eine Poetik und Hermeneutik.* Munich, 2006.

Humfress, C. 2007. *Orthodoxy and the Courts in Late Antiquity.* Oxford.

———. 2012. "Controversialist: Augustine in Combat." In Vessey 2012:323–335.

Ieraci Bio, Anna Maria. 2006. "Il dialogo nella letteratura bizantina." In Garzya 2006:21–45.

Ierodiakonou, K., ed. 2002. *Byzantine Philosophy and its Ancient Sources.* Oxford.

Ierodiakonou, K., and G. Zografidis. 2010. "Early Byzantine Philosophy." In Gerson 2010, Vol. 2: 843–868.

Inglebert, H. 2001. *Interpretatio Christiana: Les mutations des savoirs (cosmographie, géographie, ethnographie, histoire) dans l'Antiquité chrétienne, 30-600 après J.C.* Paris.

Iricinschi, E., and H. Zellentin, eds. 2008. *Heresy and Identity in Late Antiquity.* Tübingen.

Jacob, C. 2013. *The Web of Athenaeus.* Hellenic Studies 61. Washington, DC.

Jacobs, A. S. 2004. *Remains of the Jews: The Holy Land and Christian Empire in Late Antiquity.* Stanford.

———. 2007. "Dialogical Differences: (De-)Judaizing Jesus' Circumcision." *Journal of Early Christian Studies* 15:291–335.

James, L., ed. 2010. *A Companion to Byzantium.* Chichester.

Jankowiak, M. 2013. "The Invention of Dyothelitism." *Studia Patristica* 63:335–342.

Jeffreys, E., ed. 2003. *Rhetoric in Byzantium: Papers from the Thirty-Fifth Spring Symposium of Byzantine Studies, Exeter College, University of Oxford, March 2001.* Aldershot.

Johnson, S. F., ed. 2006. *Greek Literature in Late Antiquity.* Oxford.

———, ed. 2012. *The Oxford Handbook of Late Antiquity.* Oxford and New York.

———. Forthcoming. "Introduction." In *Languages and Cultures of Eastern Christianity: Greek,* ed. S. F. Johnson. Vol. 6 of *The Worlds of Eastern Christianity 300-1500.* Ed. R. Hoyland and A. Papaconstantinou. Farnham.

Kahlos, M. 2007. *Debate and Dialogue: Christian and Pagan Cultures c. 360-430.* Aldershot.

———. 2009. *Forbearance and Compulsion: The Rhetoric of Religious Tolerance and Intolerance in Late Antiquity.* London.

———, ed. 2012. *The Faces of the Other: Religious Rivalry and Ethnic Encounters in the Later Roman World.* Turnhout.

Katos, D. S. 2007. "Socratic Dialogue or Courtroom Debate? Judicial Rhetoric and Stasis Theory in the 'Dialogue on the Life of St. John Chrysostom.'" *Vigiliae Christianae* 61:42–69.

———. 2011. *Palladius of Helenopolis: The Origenist Advocate.* Oxford.

Katz, S. T., ed. 2008. *Cambridge History of Judaism* IV. Cambridge.

Kechagia, E. 2011. "Philosophy in Plutarch's 'Table-Talk': In Jest or Earnest?" In Klotz and Oikonomopoulou 2011:77–104.

Keser-Kayaalp, E., and N. Erdoğan. "The Cathedral Complex at Nisibis." *Anatolian Studies* 63:137–154.

King, D. 2012. "Why Were the Syrians Interested in Greek Philosophy?" In Wood 2012:61–81.

Klotz, F., and K. Oikonomopoulou, eds. 2011. *The Philosopher's Banquet: Plutarch's "Table-Talk" in the Intellectual Culture of the Roman Empire.* Oxford.

König, J. 2007. "Fragmentation and Coherence in Plutarch's 'Sympotic Questions.'" In König and Whitmarsh 2007:43–68.

———. 2009. "Sympotic Dialogue in the First to Fifth Centuries CE." In Goldhill 2009:85–113.

———. 2012. *Saints and Symposiasts: The Literature of Food and the Symposium in Greco-Roman and Early Christian Culture.* Cambridge.

König, J., and T. Whitmarsh, eds. 2007. *Ordering Knowledge in the Roman Empire.* Cambridge.

Kristeva, J. 1981. "Word, Dialogue and Novel." In *Desire in Language: A Semiotic Approach to Literature and Art,* ed. Leon S. Rudiez, 64–91. Oxford.

Krueger, D. 2000. "Writing and the Liturgy of Memory in Gregory of Nyssa's *Life of Macrina.*" *Journal of Early Christian Studies* 8:483–510.

———. 2003. "Writing and Redemption in the Hymns of Romanos the Melodist." *Byzantine and Modern Greek Studies* 27:1–44.

Külzer, A. 1999. *Disputationes Graecae contra Iudaeos: Untersuchungen zur byzantinischen antijüdischen Dialogliteratur und ihrem Judenbild.* Byzantinisches Archiv 18. Leipzig.

Lahey, L. 2007. "The Christian-Jewish Dialogues Through the Sixth Century (Excluding Justin)." In Skarsaune and Hvalvik 2007:581–638.

Lane, M. 2011. "Reconsidering Socratic Irony." In Morrison 2009: 237–259.

Le Boulluec, A. 1985. *La notion d'hérésie dans la littérature grecque au IIe-IIIe siècles.* 2 vols. Paris.

———. 2000. "Orthodoxie et hérésie au premiers siècles dans l'historiographie récente." In Elm 2000:303–319.

Lewis, B., and F. Niewöhner, eds. 1992. *Religionsgesprache im Mittelalter.* Wolfenbütteler Mittelalter-Studien 4. Wiesbaden.

Lieu, J. 1996. *Image and Reality: The Jews in the World of the Christians in the Second Century.* Edinburgh.

———. 2002a. *Neither Jew nor Greek.* Edinburgh.

———. 2002b. "The Forging of Christian Identity and the 'Letter to Diognetus.'" In Lieu 2002a:171–189.

———. 2002c. "'Impregnable Ramparts and Walls of Iron': Boundary and Identity in Early 'Judaism' and 'Christianity.'" *New Testament Studies* 48:297–313.

———. 2004. *Christian Identity in the Jewish and Graeco-Roman World.* Oxford.

Lieu, S. N. C. 1988. "Fact and Fiction in the *Acta Archelai.*" In Bryder 1988:69–88.

———. 1992. *Manichaeism in the Later Roman Empire and Medieval China.* 2nd ed. Tübingen.

Lim, R. 1991. "Theodoret of Cyrus and the Speakers in the Greek Dialogues." *Journal of Hellenic Studies* 111:181–182.

———. 1995a. *Public Disputation: Power and Social Order in Late Antiquity.* Berkeley.

———. 1995b. "Religious Disputation and Social Disorder in Late Antiquity." *Historia* 44:204–231.

———. 1999. "Christian Triumph and Controversy." In Brown et al. 1999:196–218.

———. 2009. "Christians, Dialogues and Patterns of Sociability in Late Antiquity." In Goldhill 2009:151–172.

Lössl, J., and J. W. Watt, eds. 2011. *Interpreting the Bible and Aristotle in Late Antiquity: The Alexandrian Commentary Tradition between Rome and Baghdad.* Farnham.

Magdalino, P. 1993. *The Empire of Manuel I Komnenos (1143–1180).* Cambridge.

Markus, R. A. 2009. "Between Marrou and Brown: Transformations of Late Antique Christianity." In Rousseau and Papoutsakis 2009:1–13

Martin, D., and P. Cox Miller, eds. 2005. *The Cultural Turn in Late Ancient Studies: Gender, Asceticism and Historiography.* Durham, NC.

Martin, J. 1931. *Symposion: Die Geschichte einer literarischen Form.* Paderborn.

Messis, C. 2012. "Public hautement affiché et public réellement visé: Le cas de l'*Apologie de l'eunuchisme* de Théophylact d'Achrida." In Odorico 2012:41–85.

Miles, R. 2009. "'Let's (Not) Talk About It': Augustine and the Control of Epistolary Dialogue." In Goldhill 2009:135–148.

Millar, F. G. B. 2007. "Theodoret of Cyrrhus: A Syrian in Greek Dress." In Amirav and Romeny 2007:105–125.

———. 2008. "Rome, Constantinople and the Near Eastern Church under Justinian: Two Synods of C.E. 536." *Journal of Roman Studies* 98:62–82.

———. 2009. "Linguistic Co-existence in Constantinople: Greek and Latin (and Syriac) in the Acts of the Synod of 536 C.E." *Journal of Roman Studies* 99:92–103.

Morbe, M. 2011. *Paulus Persa: Disputatio cum Manichaeo; Kritische tekstuitgave met inleiding.* MA thesis, Ghent University.

Moreschini, C., and E. Norelli. 2005. *Early Christian Greek and Latin Literature: A Literary History.* 2 vols. Trans. M. O'Connell. Peabody, MA. Orig. pub. as *Storia della letteratura cristiana antica greca e latina.* Brescia, 1995–1996.

Morrison, D. R., ed. 2011. *The Cambridge Companion to Socrates.* Cambridge.

Mullett, M. 1984. "Aristocracy and Patronage in the Literary Circles of Comnenian Constantinople." In Angold 1984:173–201. Repr. in Nagy 2001:409–437.

———. 2010. "Imitatio-Aemulatio-Variatio." In Rhoby and Schiffer:279–282.

Munitiz, J. A. 1988. "Catechetical Teaching-aids in Byzantium." In Chrysostomides 1988:69–83.

Munnich, O. 2012. "La place de l'hellénisme dans l'autodéfinition du christianisme: L'*Apologie* de Justin." In Perrot 2012:61–122.

Murdoch, I. 1977. *The Fire and the Sun: Why Plato Banished the Artists; Based on the Romanes Lecture 1976*. Oxford. Repr. London, 1990.

———. 1986. *Acastos: Two Platonic Dialogues*. London.

Murray, O., ed. 1995. *Sympotica: A Symposium on the Symposium*. Oxford.

Nagy, G., ed. 2001. *Greek Literature in the Byzantine Period*. Vol. 9 of *Greek Literature*. Ed. G. Nagy. New York.

Niehoff, M. R. 2008. "Questions and Answers in Philo and Genesis Rabbah." *Journal for the Study of Judaism* 39:337–366.

Nilsson, I. 2010. "The Same Story, but Another: A Reappraisal of Literary Imitation in Byzantium." In Rhoby and Schiffer 2010:195–208.

Noble, T. X., and J. M. Smith, eds. 2008. *Early Medieval Christianities, c. 600–c. 1100*. Vol. 3 of *Cambridge History of Christianity*. Ed. T. F. X. Noble and J. M. H Smith. Cambridge.

Noret, J. 1999. "La rédaction de la Disputatio cum Pyrrho (CPG 7698) de saint Maxime le Confesseur, serait-il postérieure à 655?" *Analecta Bollandiana* 117:291–296.

Nygren, A. 1953. *Eros and Agape: A Study of the Christian Idea of Love*. Rev. ed. London.

Odorico, P., ed. 2012. *La face cachée de la littérature byzantine, le texte en tant que message immédiat: Actes du colloque international, Paris, 5-6-7 juin 2008 organisé par Paolo Odorico en mémoire de Constantin Leventis*. Paris.

Olajos, T. 1981. "Contributions à la genèse de l'Histoire universelle de Théophylacte Simocatta." *Acta Antiqua Academiae Scientarum Hungaricae* 29:417–418.

O'Meara, D. 2002. "The Justinianic Dialogue 'On Political Science' and its Neoplatonic Sources." In Ierodiakonou 2002:49–62.

———. 2003. *Platonopolis: Platonic Political Philosophy in Late Antiquity*. Oxford.

Oikonomopoulou, K. 2011. "Peripatetic Knowledge in Plutarch's Table-Talk." In Klotz and Oikonomopoulou 2011:105–130.

Olster, D. 1994. *Roman Defeat, Christian Response and the Literary Construction of the Jew*. Philadelphia.

Papadogiannakis (Papadoyannakis), Y. 2006. "Instruction by Question and Answer: The Case of Late Antique and Byzantine 'erotapokriseis.'" In Johnson 2006:92–102.

———. 2008a. "A Debate about the Rebuilding of the Temple in Sixth-Century Byzantium." In Gardner and Osterloh 2008:373–382.

———. 2008b. "Defining Orthodoxy in Pseudo-Justin's 'Quaestiones et responsiones ad orthodoxos.'" In Iricinschi and Zellentin 2008:115–127.

———. 2012. *Christianity and Hellenism in the Fifth-Century Greek East: Theodoret's Apologetics against the Greeks in Context.* Hellenic Studies 49. Washington, DC.

Patterson, L. G. 1997. *Methodius of Olympus: Divine Sovereignty, Human Freedom, and Life in Christ.* Cambridge, MA.

Penella, R. 2013. "Prologue." In Quiroga Puertas 2013:1–7.

Perelman, C. 1982. *The Realm of Rhetoric.* Trans. W. Kluback. Notre Dame, IN. Orig. pub. as *L'empire rhétorique.*

Perelman, C., and L. Olbrechts-Tyteca. 1969. *The New Rhetoric: A Treatise in Argumentation.* Trans. J. Wilkinson and P. Weaver. Notre Dame, IN.

Pernot, L. 1993a. "Un rendez-vous manqué." *Rhetorica* 11:421–434.

———. 1993b. *La rhétorique de l'éloge dans le monde gréco-romain.* 2 vols. Paris.

Perrot, A., ed. 2012. *Les chrétiens et l'hellénisme: Identités religieuses et culture grecque dans l'Antiquité tardive.* Paris.

Price, R., and Mary Whitby, eds. 2009. *Chalcedon in Context: Church Councils 400–700.* Liverpool.

Quiroga (Puertas), A. 2007. "From 'Sophistopolis' to 'Episcopolis': The Case for a Third Sophistic." *Journal for Late Antique Religion and Culture* 1:31–42.

———, ed. 2013. *The Purpose of Rhetoric in Late Antiquity: From Performance to Exegesis.* Studien und Texte zu Antike und Christentum 72. Tübingen.

Rajak, T. 1999. "Talking at Trypho: Christian Apologetic as Anti-Judaism in Justin's Dialogue with Trypho the Jew." In *Apologetics in the Roman Empire: Pagans, Jews and Christians,* ed. M. J. Edwards, M. D. Goodman and S. R. F. Price, 59–80. Oxford.

Ramelli, I. R. 2009b. *Bardaisan of Edessa: A Reassessment of the Evidence and a New Interpretation.* Piscataway, NJ. (For Ramelli 2009a, see above, Editions and Translations of Primary Sources.)

Reinink, G. J. 1991. "Ein syrisch Streitgespräch zwischen Tod und Satan." In Reinink and Vanstiphout 1991:135–152.

———. 1999. "Babai the Great's 'Life of George' and the Propagation of Doctrine in the Late Sassanian Empire." In Drijvers and Watt 1999:171–193.

Reinink, G. J., and H. L. J. Vanstiphout, eds. 1991. *Dispute Poems and Dialogues in the Ancient and Mediaeval Near East: Forms and Types of Literary Debates in Semitic and Related Literatures.* Orientalia Lovaniensia Analecta 42. Leuven.

Richard, M. 1951. "Les florilèges diphysites du Ve et du VIe siècles." In *Das Konzil von Chalkedon* I, ed. A. Grillmeier and H. Bacht, 721–748. Würzburg.

———. 2011. "Diophysite Florilegia of the Fifth and Sixth Centuries CE." In Cameron and Hoyland 2011:321–346. English trans. of Richard 1951.

Rhoby, A., and E. Schiffer, eds. 2010. *Imitatio, Aemulatio, Variatio: Akten des internationalen wissenschaftlichen Symposions zur byzantinischen Sprache und Literatur (Wien, 22-25. Oktober 2008)*. Vienna.

Robin, C. 2012. "Ethiopia and Arabia." In Johnson 2012:247–332.

———. Forthcoming. "The Peoples Beyond the Arabian Frontier in Late Antiquity: Recent Epigraphic Discoveries and Latest Advances." In Dijkstra and Fisher, forthcoming.

Ronconi, F. 2012. "La collection brisée: La face cachée de la 'collection philosophique'; Les milieux socioculturelles." In Odorico 2012:137–166.

Rosenqvist, J. O., ed. 2004. *Interaction and Isolation in Late Byzantine Culture*. Stockholm.

Rossetti, L. 1989. "The Rhetoric of Socrates." *Philosophy and Rhetoric* 22:225–238.

———. 1997. "Arguing and Suggesting within a Platonic Dialogue: Towards a Typology." In Hart and Tejera 1997:215–245.

———. 2007. "A Context for Plato's Dialogues." In Bosch-Veciana and Montserrat-Molas 2007:15–31.

———. 2011. "Un Socrate che non ascolta: Per esempio nell'Eutifrone." *Peitho* I:25–38.

Rousseau, P., and M. Papoutsakis, eds. 2009. *Transformations of Late Antiquity: Essays for Peter Brown*. Aldershot.

Runia, D. T. 1989. "Festugière Revisited: Aristotle in the Greek Patres." *Vigiliae Christianae* 43:1–34.

Saïd, S., and M. Trédé. 1999. *A Short History of Greek Literature*. 1999.

Saliou, C., ed. 2010. *Gaza dans l'Antiquité Tardive: Archéologie, rhétorique, histoire.* Salerno.

Sansterre, J. -M. 1983. *Les moines grecs et orientaux à Rome aux époques byzantine et carolingienne (milieu du VIe s. - fin du IXe s.)*. Brussels.

Sarris, P. et al., eds. 2011. *An Age of Saints? Power, Conflict and Dissent in Early Medieval Christianity*. Leiden.

Schamp, J. 2006. "Sophistes à l'ambon: Esquisses pour la Troisième Sophistique comme paysage littéraire." In Amato 2006:286–338.

Schmidt, P. L. 1977. "Zur Typologie und Literarisierung des frühchristlichen lateinischen Dialogs." In Alan Cameron 1977:101–190.

Schor, A. M. 2011. *Theodoret's People: Social Networks and Religious Conflict in Late Roman Syria*. Berkeley.

Schörner, G., and D. Erker Sterbenc, eds. 2008. *Medien religiöser Kommunikationen im Imperium Romanum*. Potsdamer Altertumswissenschaftliche Beiträge 24. Stuttgart.

Schreckenberg, H. 1999. *Die christlichen Adversus-Iudaeos-Texte und ihr literarisches und historisches Umfeld (1-11 Jh.).* 4th ed. Frankfurt am Main.

Schrenk, L., ed. 1994. *Aristotle in Late Antiquity.* Washington, DC.

Schurig, S. 2005. *Die Theologie des Kreuzes beim frühen Cyrill von Alexandria.* Tübingen.

Shahid, I. 1979. "Byzantium in South Arabia." *Dumbarton Oaks Papers* 33:23–94.

Siniossoglou, N. 2008. *Plato and Theodoret: The Christian Appropriation of Platonic Philosophy and the Hellenic Intellectual Resistance.* Cambridge.

Sizgorich, T. 2009. *Violence and Belief in Late Antiquity: Militant Devotion in Christianity and Islam.* Philadelphia.

Skarsaune, O. 1987. *The Proof from Prophecy: A Study in Justin Martyr's Proof-Text Tradition; Text-Type, Provenance, Theological Profile.* Leiden.

Skarsaune, O., and R. Hvalvik, eds. 2007. *Jewish Believers in Jesus: The Early Centuries* I. Peabody, MA.

Smith, A., ed. 2005. *The Philosopher and Society in Late Antiquity.* Swansea.

Smith, P. C. 1997. "Tensions in the 'Phaedrus': Dialogue and Dialectic, Speech and Writing." In Hart and Tejera 1997:169–199.

Smith, D. E. 2003. *From Symposium to Eucharist: The Banquet in the Early Christian World.* Philadelphia.

Snyder, J. R. 1989. *Writing the Scene of Speaking: Theories of Dialogue in the Late Italian Renaissance.* Stanford.

Stock, B. 2010. *Augustine's Inner Dialogue: The Philosophical Soliloquy in Late Antiquity.* Cambridge.

Stroumsa, S., and G. G. Stroumsa. 1988. "Aspects of Anti-Manichaean Polemic in Late Antiquity and under Early Islam." *Harvard Theological Review* 81:37–58.

Tambrun-Krasker, B. 2006. *Pléthon: Le retour de Platon.* Paris.

———. 2012. "Byzance, Platon et les platoniciens." *Platon et l'Orient.* Brussels. Accessed July 24, 2013. http://halshs.archives-ouvertes.fr/halshs-00735103/.

Tannous, J. 2013. "'You Are What You Read': Qenneshre and the Miaphysite Church in the Seventh Century." In Wood 2013a:83–102.

Urbainczyk, T. 2002. *Theodoret of Cyrrhus: The Bishop and the Holy Man.* Ann Arbor, MI.

Uthemann, K.-H. 1981a. "Syllogistik im Dienst der Orthodoxie: Zwei unedierte Texte byzantinischer Kontroverstheologie des 6. Jahrhunderts." *Jahrbuch der Österreichischen Byzantinistik* 30:103–112.

———. 1981b. "Des Patriarchen Anastasius I von Antiochien Jerusalemer Streitgespräch mit einen Tritheiten (CPG 6958)." *Traditio* 37:73–107.

Van Deun, P. 2009. "Développements récents des recherches sur Maxime le Confesseur (1998–2009)." *Sacris Eruditi* 48:97–167.

Van Deun, P., and C. Macé, eds. 2011. *Encyclopaedic Trends in Byzantium.* Leuven.

Van Hoof, L. 2010. "Greek Rhetoric and the Later Roman Empire: The Bubble of the 'Third Sophistic.'" *Antiquité tardive* 18:211–224.

Van Moos, P. 1989. "Le dialogue latin au Moyen Âge: L'exemple d'Evrard d'Ypres." *Annales: Économies, Sociétés, Civilisations* 44.4:993–1028.

Van Nuffelen, P. 2013. "Palladius and the Johannite Schism." *Journal of Ecclesiastical History* 64:1–19.

———. 2014. "The End of Open Competition? Religious Disputations in Late Antiquity." In Engels and Van Nuffelen 2014.

Vessey, M., ed. 2012. *A Companion to Augustine*. With the assistance of S. Reid. Oxford.

Volgers, A., and C. Zamagni, eds. 2004. *Erotapokriseis: Early Christian Question and Answer Literature in Context*. Leuven.

Voss, B. R. 1970. *Der Dialog in der frühchristlichen Literatur*. Münster.

Walker, J. T. 2006. *The Legend of Mar Qardagh: Narrative and Christian Heroism in Late Antique Iraq*. Berkeley.

Watt, J. W. 2010. *Rhetoric and Philosophy from Greek into Syriac*. Farnham.

Watts, E. J. 2005a. "Winning the Intracommunal Dialogues: Zacharias Scholasticus' 'Life of Severus.'" *Journal of Early Christian Studies* 13:437–464.

———. 2005b. "An Alexandrian Christian Response to Fifth-Century Neoplatonic Influence." In Smith 2005: 215–229.

———. 2006. *City and School in Late Antique Athens and Alexandria*. Berkeley.

———. 2006–2007. "Creating the Ascetic and Sophistic Mélange: Zacharias Scholasticus and the Intellectual Influence of Aeneas of Gaza and John Rufus." *Aram* 18–19:153–164.

Weber, D. 2000. "Dialogue." In Döpp and Gerlings 2000:168–169.

Wessel, S. 2010. "Memory and Individuality in Gregory of Nyssa's 'De anima et resurrectione.'" *Journal of Early Christian Studies* 18:369–392.

Wickham, L. R. 2012. Review of Schor 2001. *Journal of Theological Studies* 63:335–337.

Wickham, L. R., and C. P. Bammel, eds. 1993. *Christian Faith and Greek Philosophy in Late Antiquity: Essays in Tribute to George Christopher Stead*. Leiden.

Whitby, Mary. 2010. "Rhetorical Questions." In James 2010:239–250.

Whitby, Michael. 1988. *The Emperor Maurice and his Historian: Theophylact Simocatta on Persian and Balkan Warfare*. Oxford.

Williams, R. 1993. "Macrina's Deathbed Revisited: Gregory of Nyssa on Mind and Passion." In Wickham and Bammel 1993:227–246.

Wimbush, V. L., and R. Valantasis, eds. 1995. *Asceticism*. New York.

Winkelmann, F. 1987. "Die Quellen zur Erforschung des monenergetisch-monotheletischen Streites." *Klio* 69:515–559.

———. 2001. *Der monenergetisch-monotheletische Streit*. Frankfurt am Main.

Wilson, K. F. 1985. *Incomplete Fictions: The Formation of English Renaissance Dialogue.* Washington, DC.

Wilson, N. G. 1970. "Indications of Speaker in Greek Dialogue Texts." *Classical Quarterly* 20:305.

Wood, P. 2010. *"We Have no King but Christ": Christian Political Thought in Greater Syria on the Eve of the Arab Conquest (c. 400–585).* Oxford.

———. 2013a. "The 'Chronicle of Seert' and Roman Ecclesiastical History in the Sasanian World." In Wood 2013b:43–59.

———, ed. 2013b. *History and Identity in the Late Antique Near East.* Oxford.

Young, F. 1983. *From Nicaea to Chalcedon.* London.

———. 1997. *Biblical Exegesis and the Formation of Christian Culture.* Cambridge.

Young, F. et al., eds. 2004. *Cambridge History of Early Christian Literature.* Cambridge.

Zorzi, M. B. 2003. "Castità e generazione nel bello: L'eros nel Simposio di Metodio d'Olimpo." *Mneme.* Accessed July 23, 2013. http://mondodomani.org/reportata/zorzi02.htm.

———. 2003. *La personalità delle vergini e l'epilogo del Simposio di Metodio d'Olimpo: Una critic all'encratismo.* Accessed July 23, 2013. http://mondodomani.org/reportata/zorzi03.htm.

Index

CPSIA information can be obtained at www.ICGtesting.com
Printed in the USA
BVOW02s1522140115

382430BV00009B/14/P